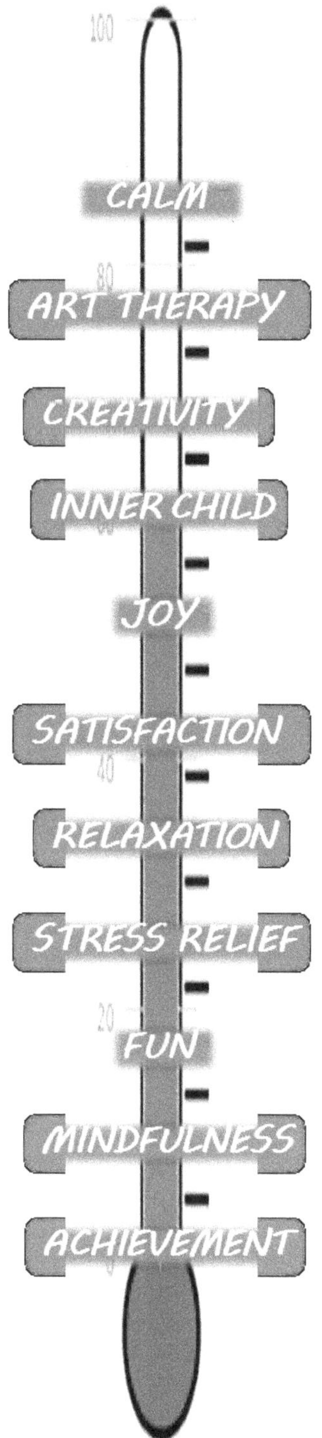

Getting started...

Each page is printed only on the right hand side. It helps stop bleeding or hand pressure affecting the next drawing.

Colored pencils and crayons are fine to use.

If you are planning to use wet markers, pens or watercolor paint, please place a sheet of paper or cardboard under your current page. It's also a good idea to avoid excessive wetness.

Start on any page you like. There's no fixed order.

Enjoying the process...

Just relax and have fun with the coloring process.

It's OK to:

- ✓ Add your own creative lines or drawings.
- ✓ Add color outside lines for contrast effect.
- ✓ Leave areas uncolored for creative effect.

Sharing this coloring book...

Sharing with your grandchildren or children enhances the creative experience and relationship for you both.

Artists and Writers ...

Often lose track of time and awareness outside of their work. If you should suddenly become aware of this sensation take notice of how calm and unstressed you are. Acknowledge the joy, the inner child, the creativity and keep coloring.

"Be yourself; -
everyone else is
already taken."

— Oscar Wilde

50 Magical Mandalas VOL 1

Easy to complex designs
with notes, quotes & jokes
For both kids and adults to color

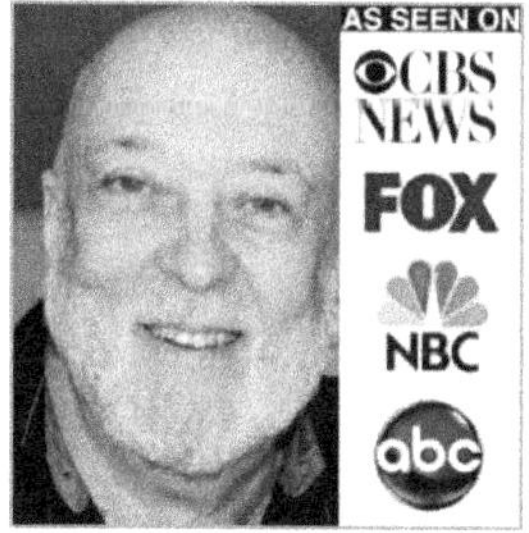

Richard Wineberg
Life Coach, Artist, Author, Publisher, Dancer, Grandfather

Imagine dancing to the rhythm of your own life, not stuck in any rut, not tripping over two left feet, knowing what you want and choosing to live your Purpose from the inside out.

It is my wish that you should taste, feel and be your Purpose.

Coloring books are a great form of art therapy to help the process. Let go of stress, relax, find your inner child and creativity and grow your sense of joy.

Remember, it's always time to dance...

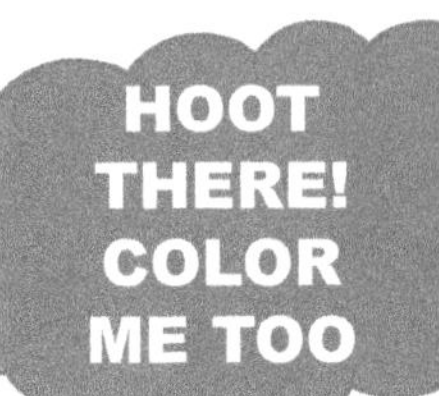

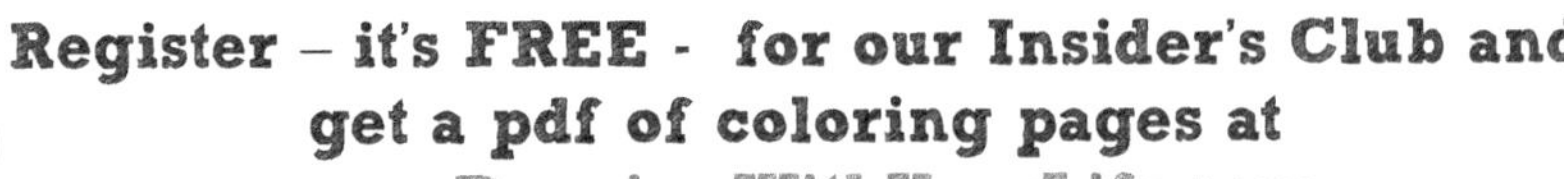

1 **Register – it's FREE - for our Insider's Club and get a pdf of coloring pages at**
www.DancingWithYourLife.com
And check out the full range of our books and products while you're there.

****

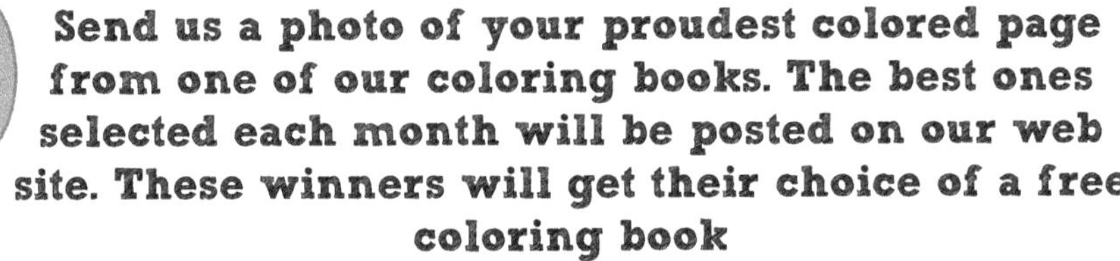

2 **Send us a photo of your proudest colored page from one of our coloring books. The best ones selected each month will be posted on our web site. These winners will get their choice of a free coloring book**
Email: support@DancingWithYourLife.com

****

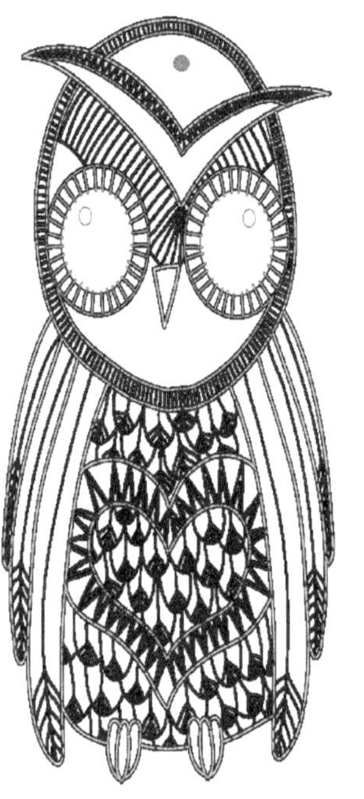

3 **Please leave a review to let us know how you went with this book**

ISBN 978-0-9944230-2-3

Published by Seshat Publications
13/56 Carl Street, Woolloongabba Qld 4102 Australia
Web: www.SeshatPublications.com
Email: Support@SeshatPublishing.com

Printed by CreateSpace

Compilation and design by Richard Wineberg
Email: rkw@RichardWineberg.com

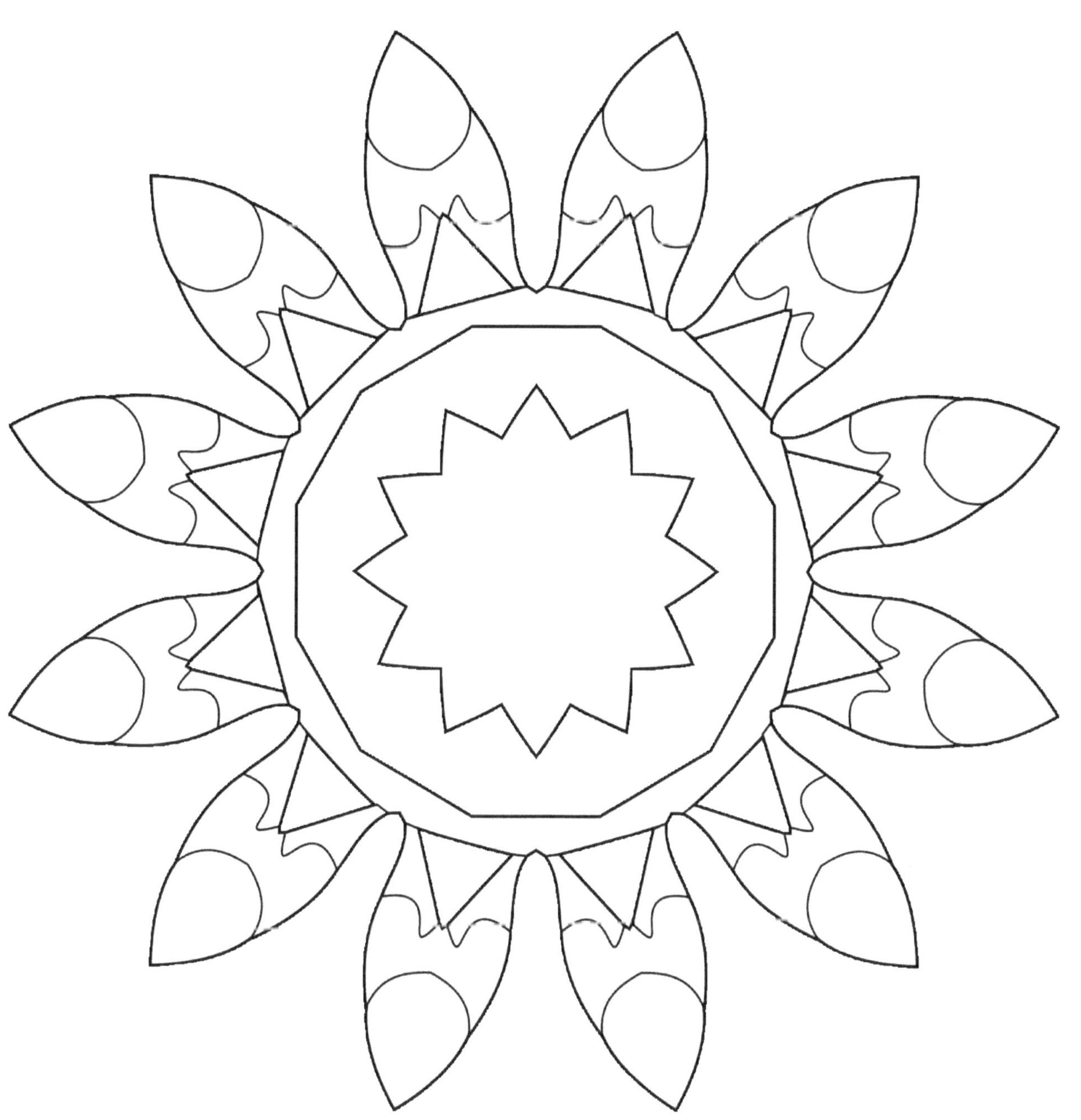

"You've gotta
dance like there's
nobody watching,
Love like you'll
never be hurt,
Sing like there's
nobody listening,
And live like it's
heaven on earth."

— William W. Purkey

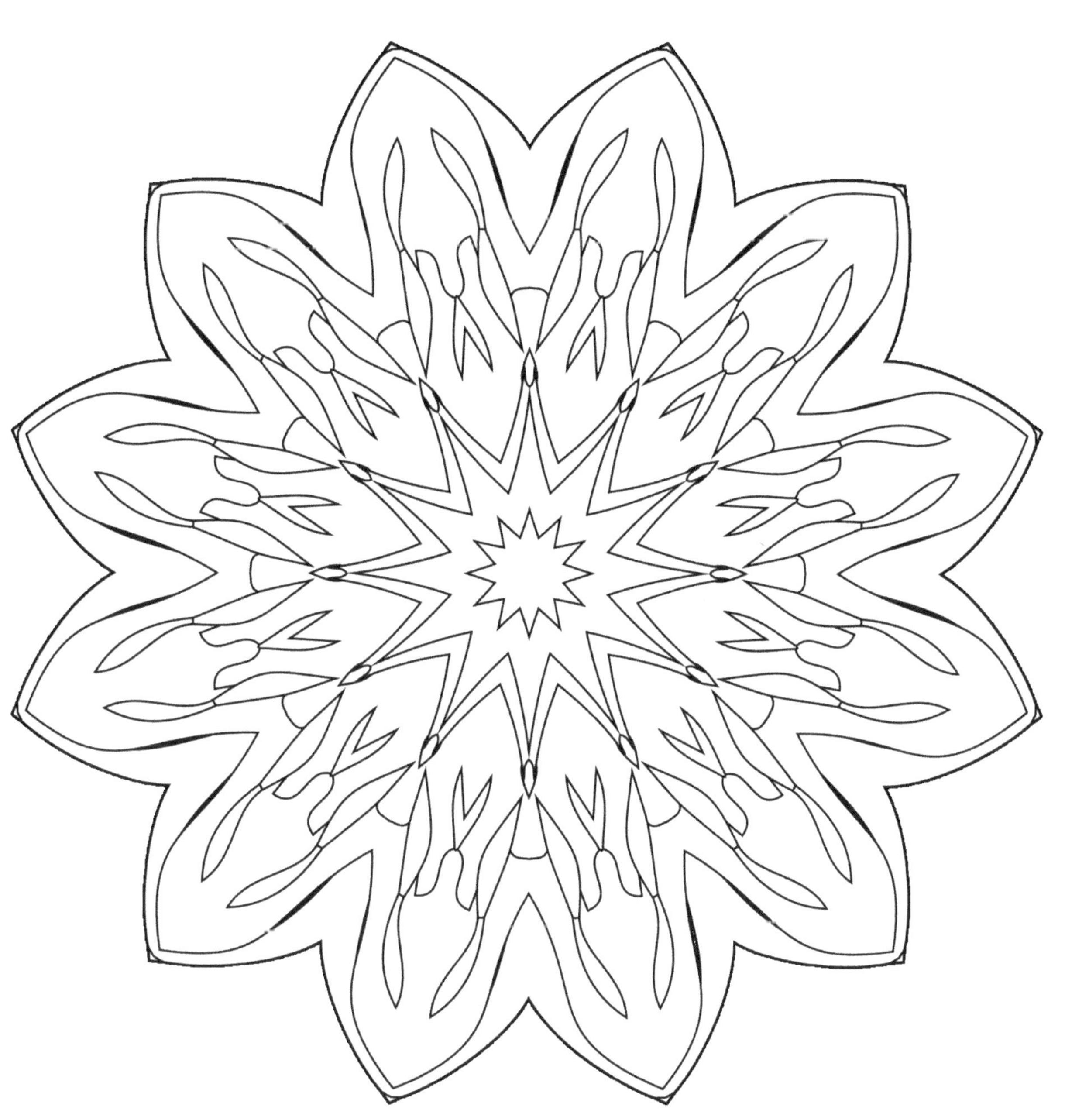

"Be the change that you wish to see in the world."

— Mahatma Gandhi

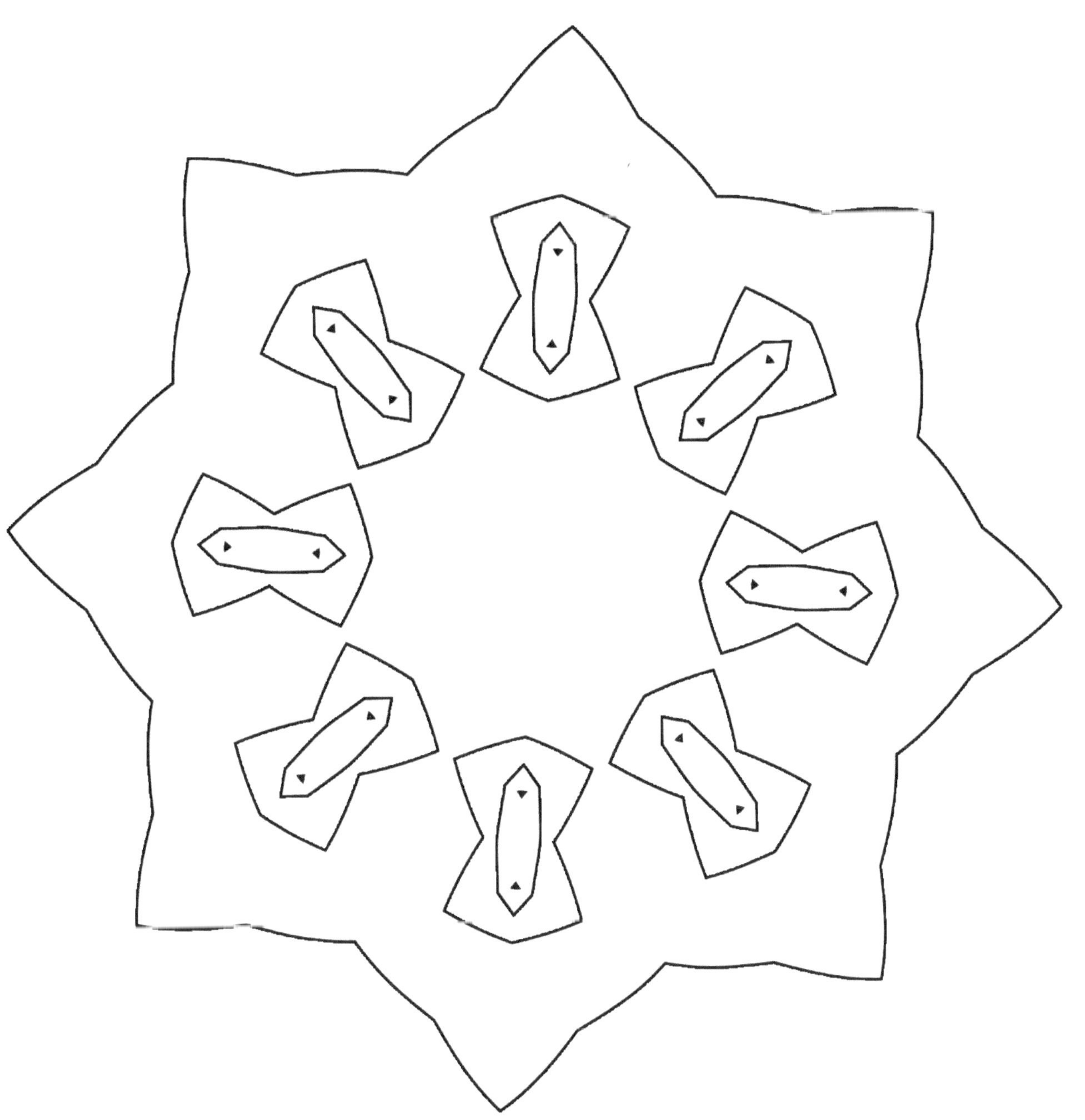

"No one can make you feel inferior without your consent."

— Eleanor Roosevelt, This is My Story

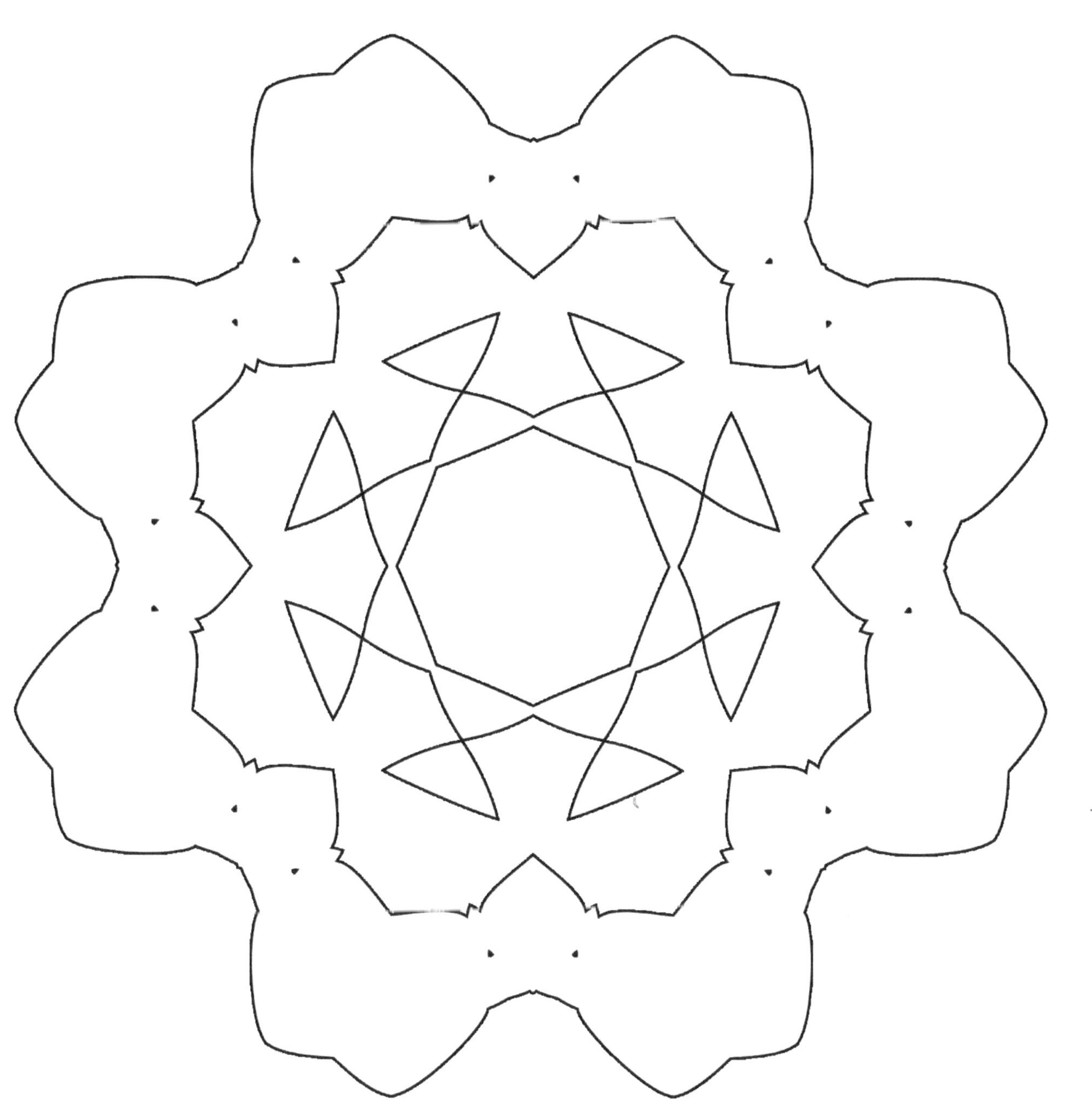

"Live as if you were
to die tomorrow.
Learn as if you
were to live
forever."

— Mahatma Gandhi

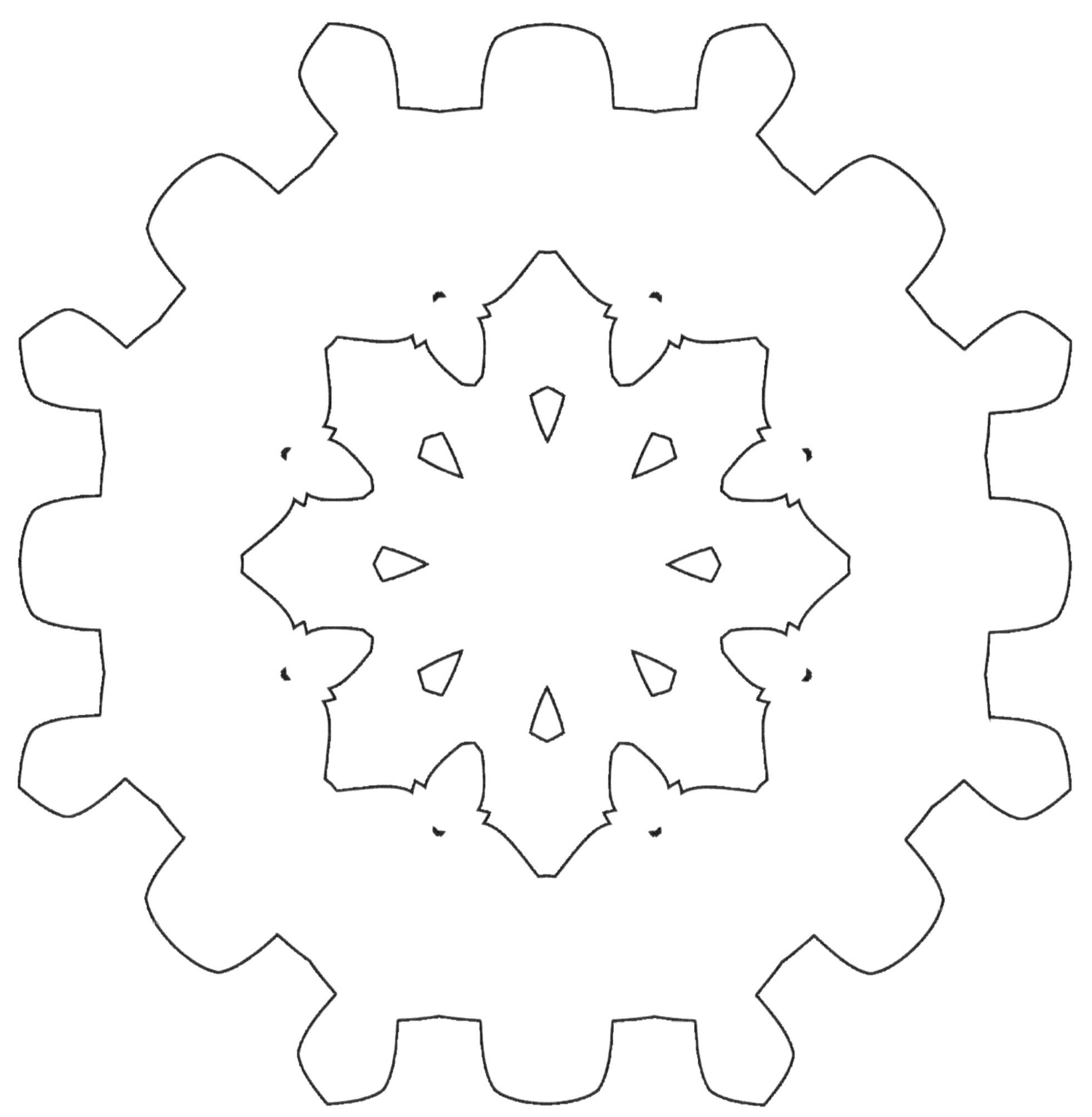

"Darkness cannot drive out darkness: only light can do that. Hate cannot drive out hate: only love can do that."

— Martin Luther King Jr., A Testament of Hope: The Essential Writings and Speeches

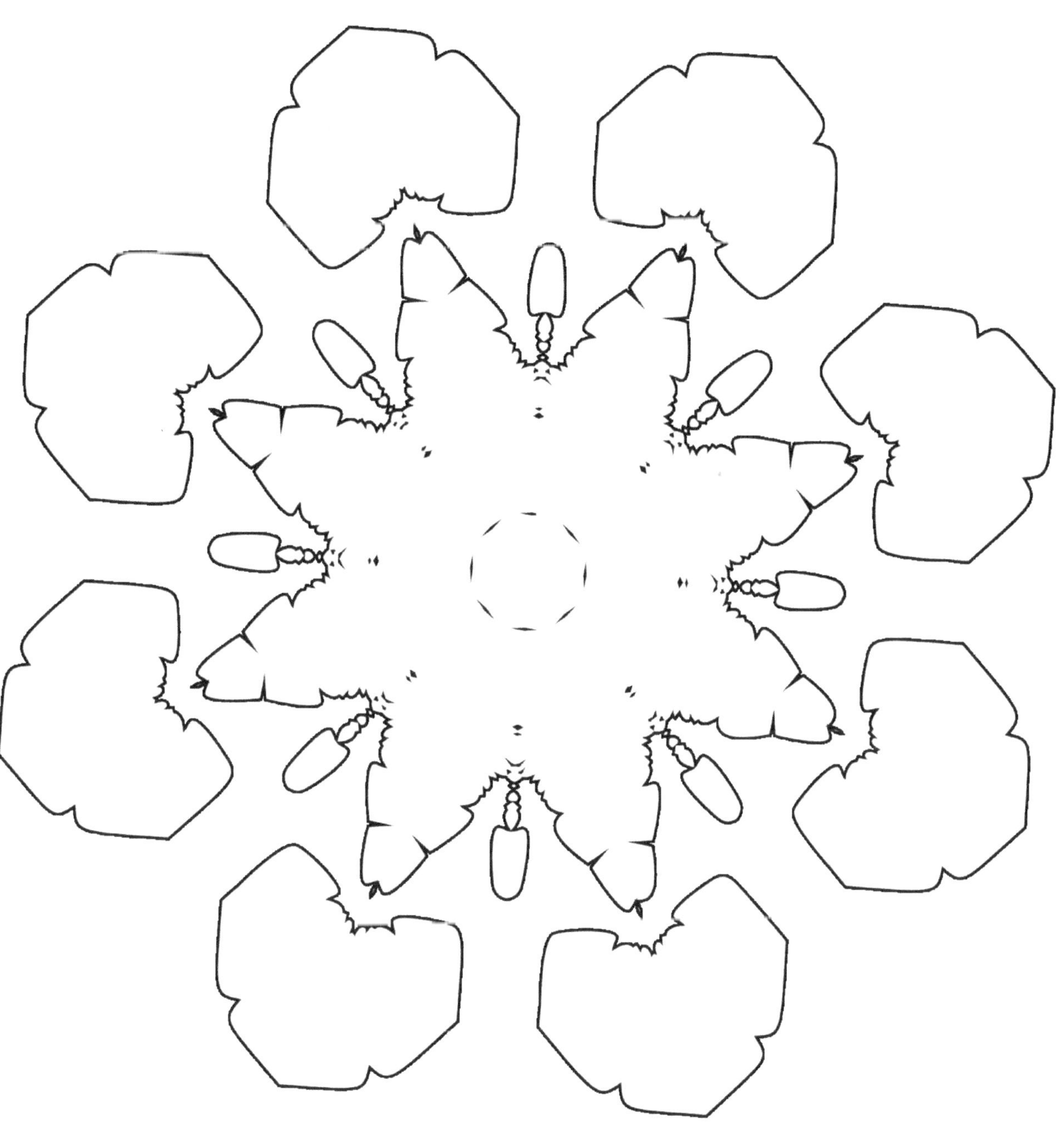

"Without music,
life would be a
mistake."

— Friedrich Nietzsche, Twilight of the Idols

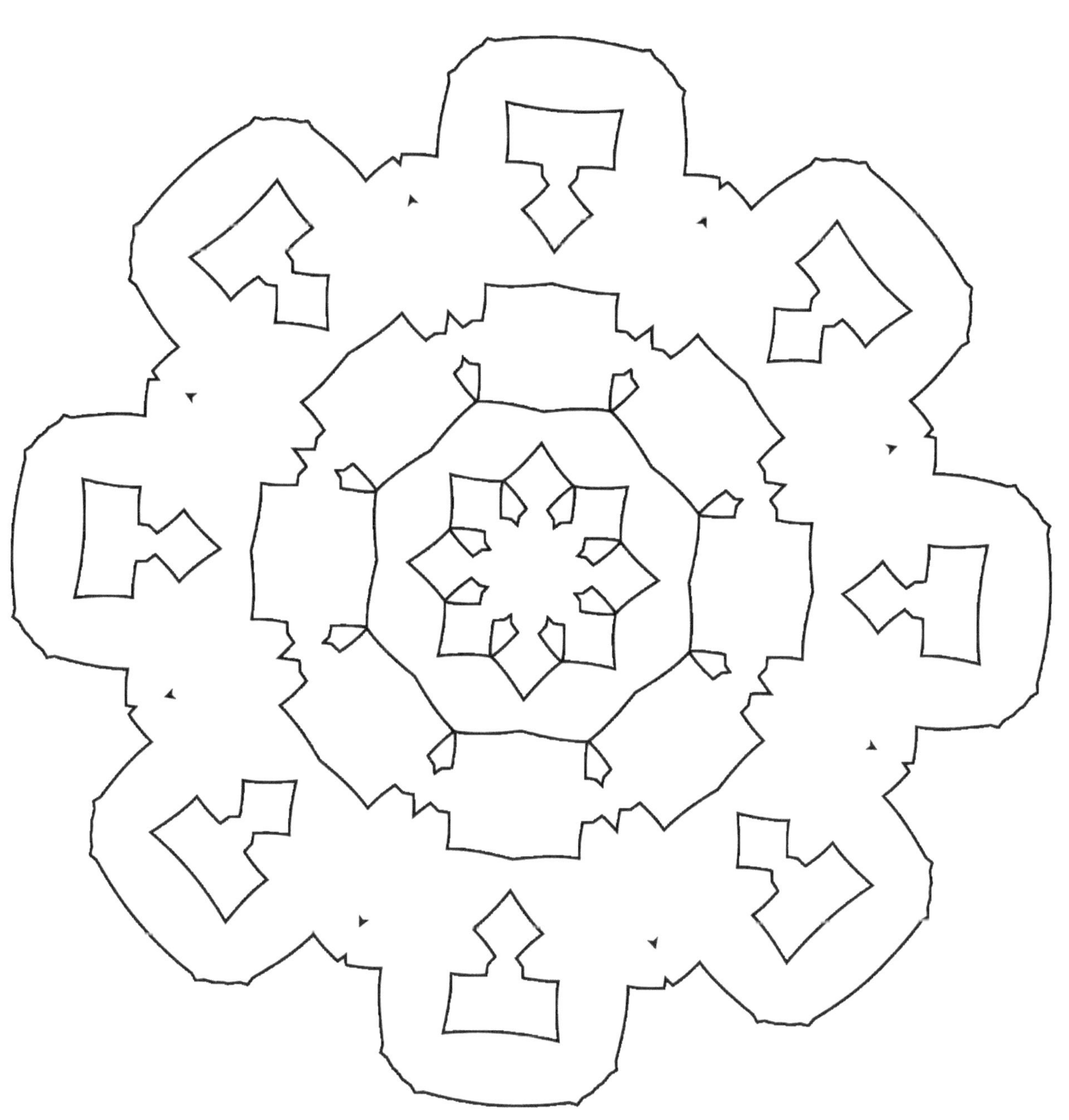

"We accept the love we think we deserve."

— Stephen Chbosky, The Perks of Being a Wallflower

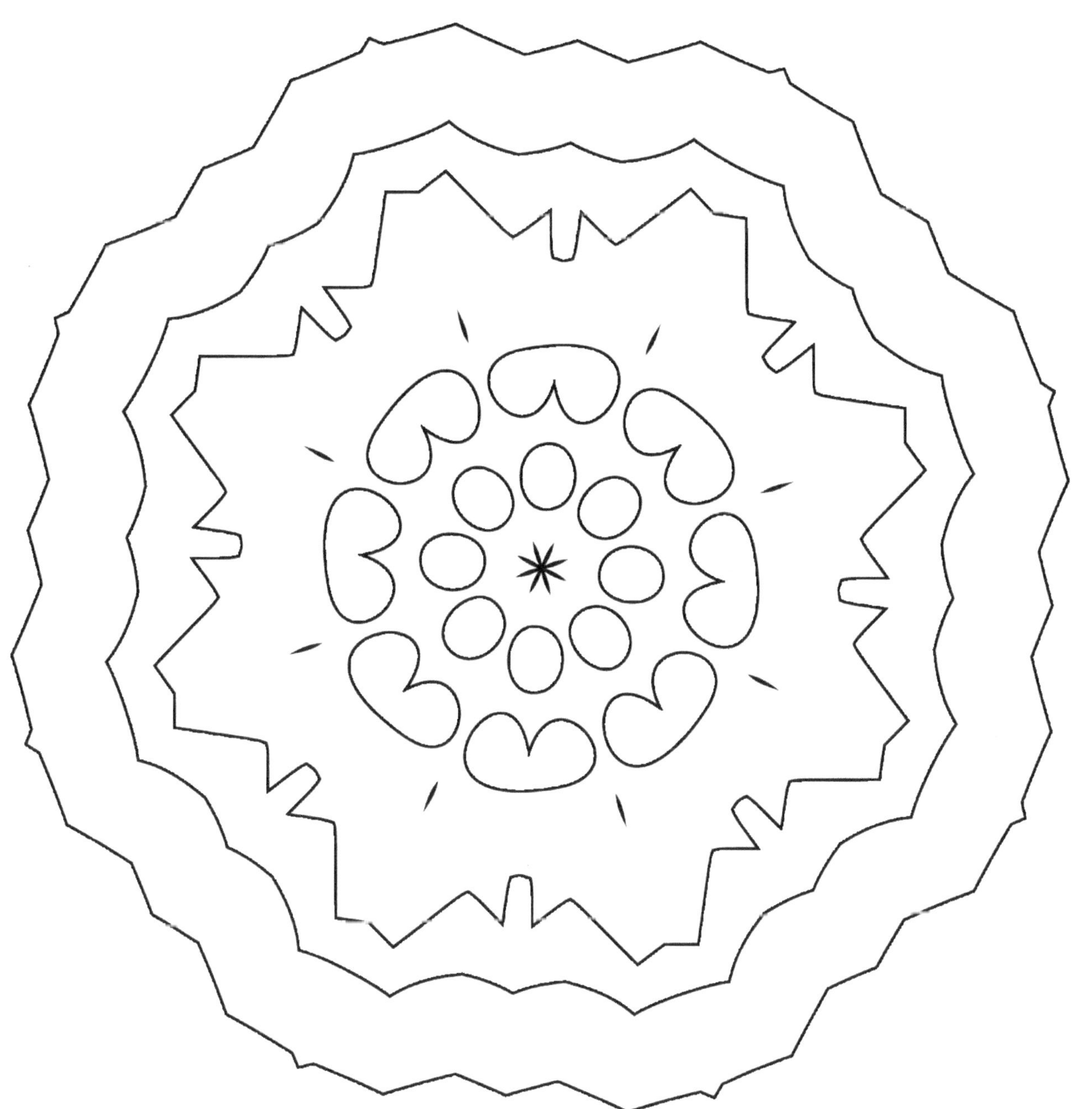

"Imperfection is beauty, madness is genius and it's better to be absolutely ridiculous than absolutely boring."

— Marilyn Monroe

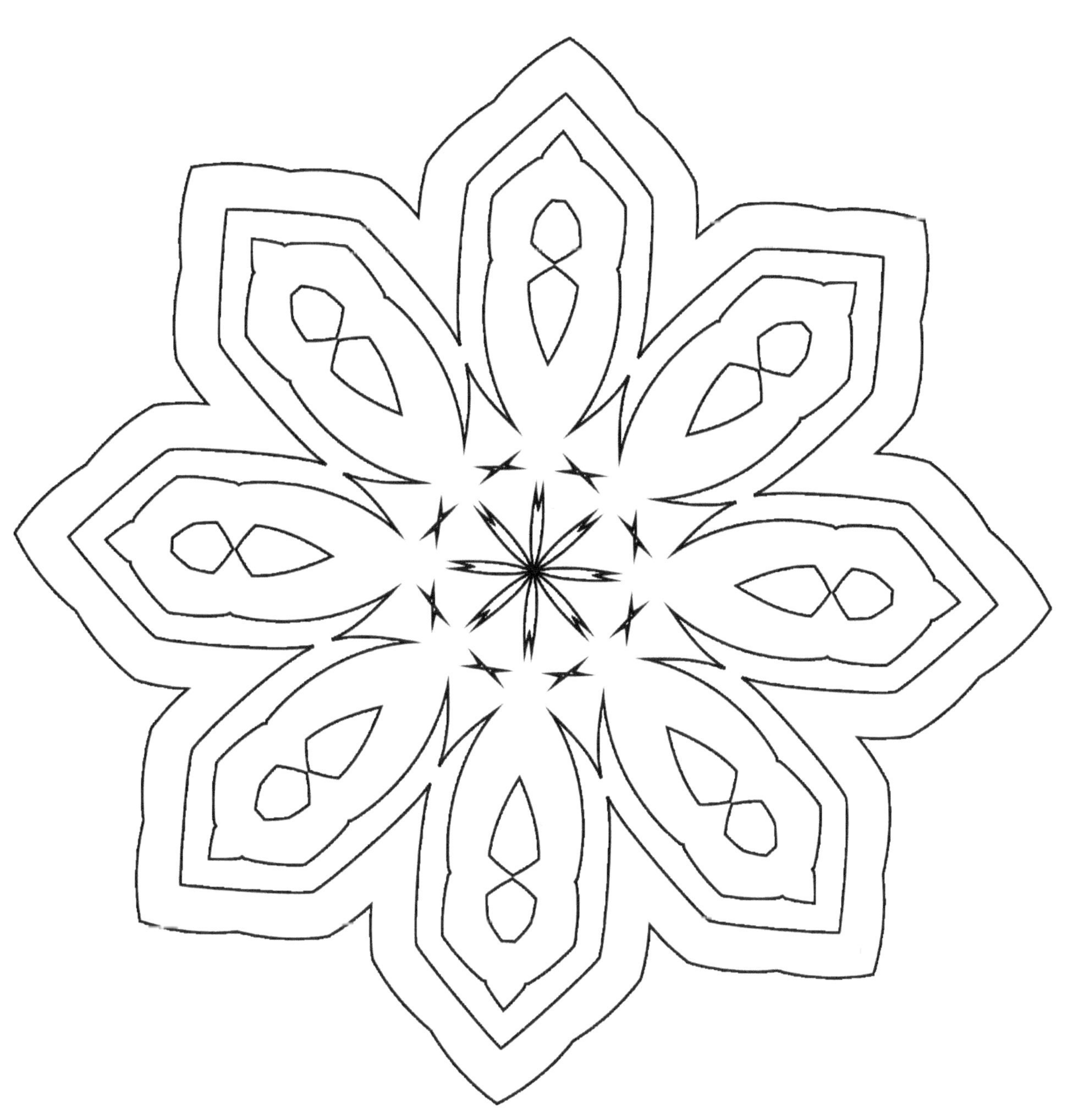

"There are only two ways to live your life. One is as though nothing is a miracle. The other is as though everything is a miracle."

— Albert Einstein

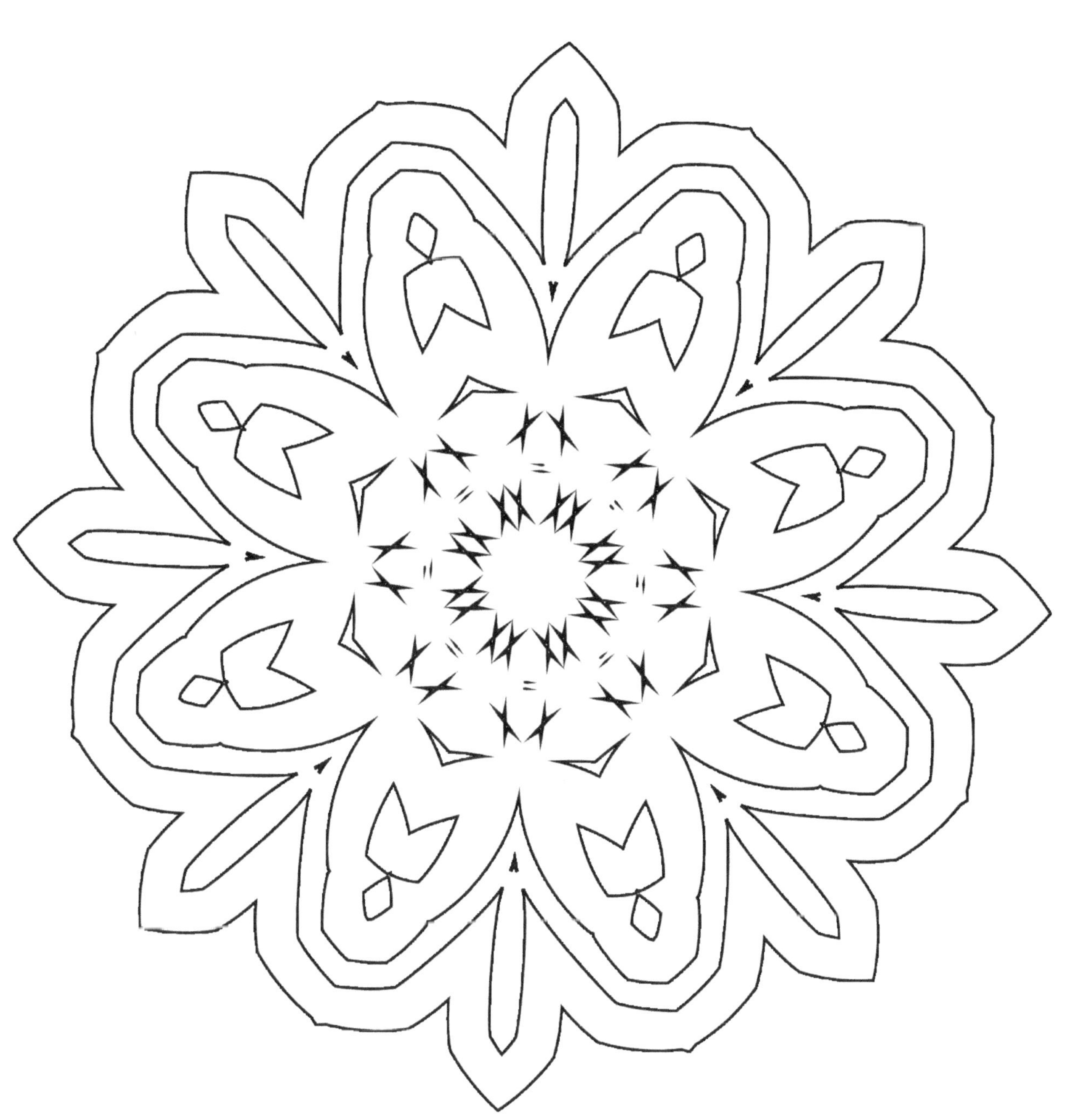

"Yesterday is
history, tomorrow
is a mystery,
today is a gift of
God, which is why
we call it the
present."

— Bill Keane

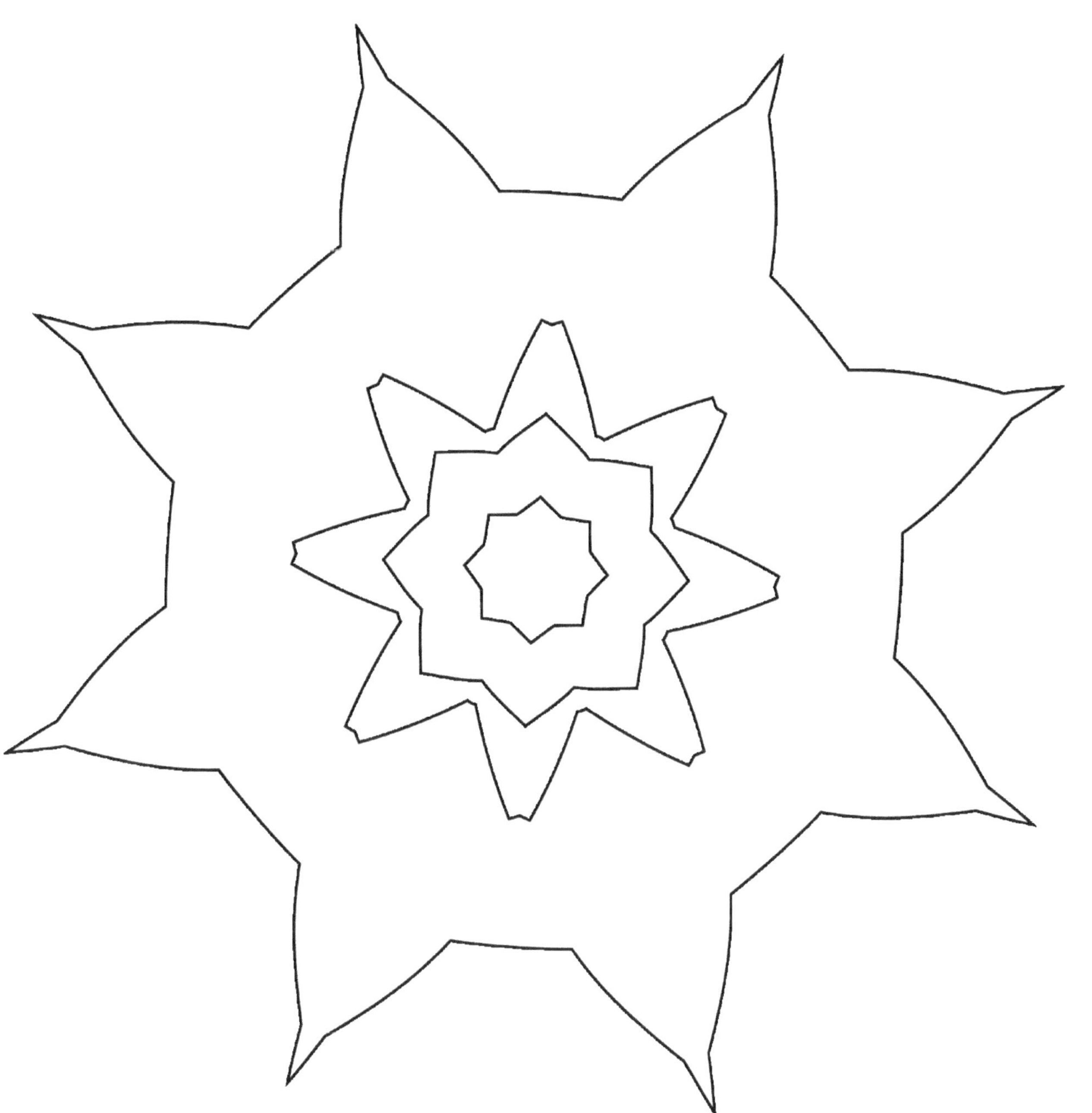

"We are all in the gutter, but some of us are looking at the stars."

— Oscar Wilde, Lady Windermere's Fan

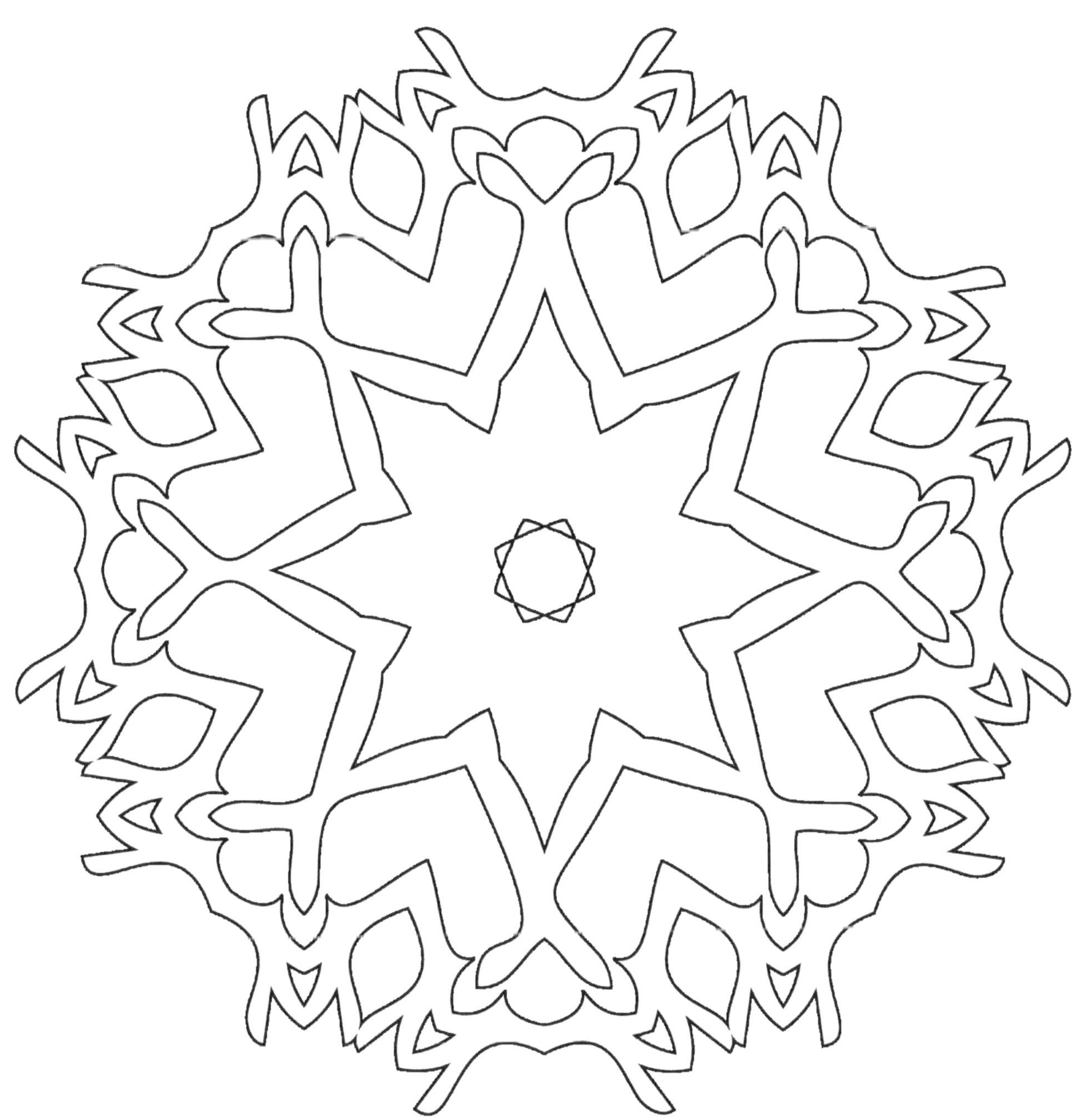

“I have not failed. I've just found 10,000 ways that won't work.”

— Thomas A. Edison

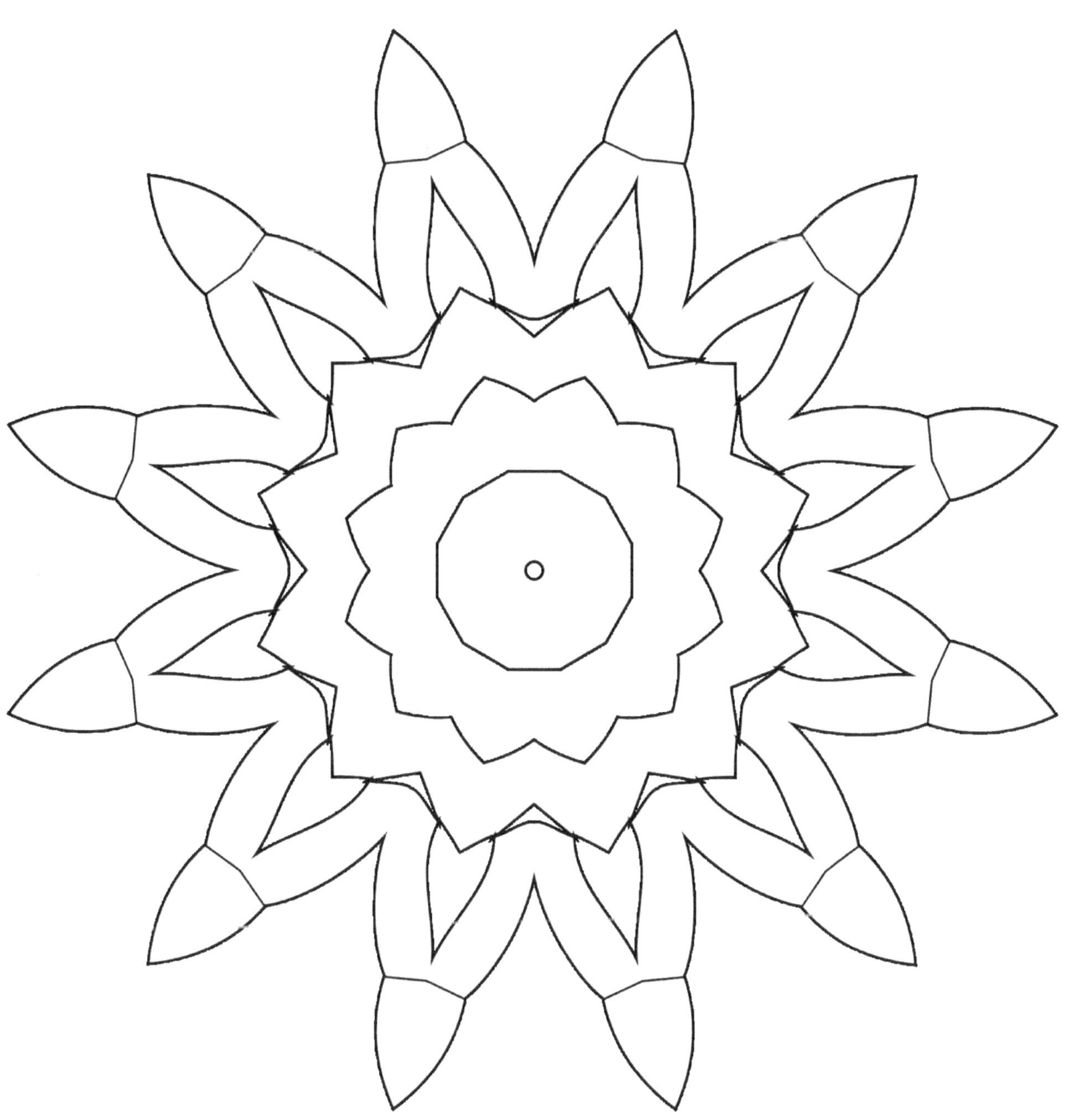

"The opposite of love is not hate, it's indifference. The opposite of art is not ugliness, it's indifference. The opposite of faith is not heresy, it's indifference. And the opposite of life is not death, it's indifference."

— Elie Wiesel

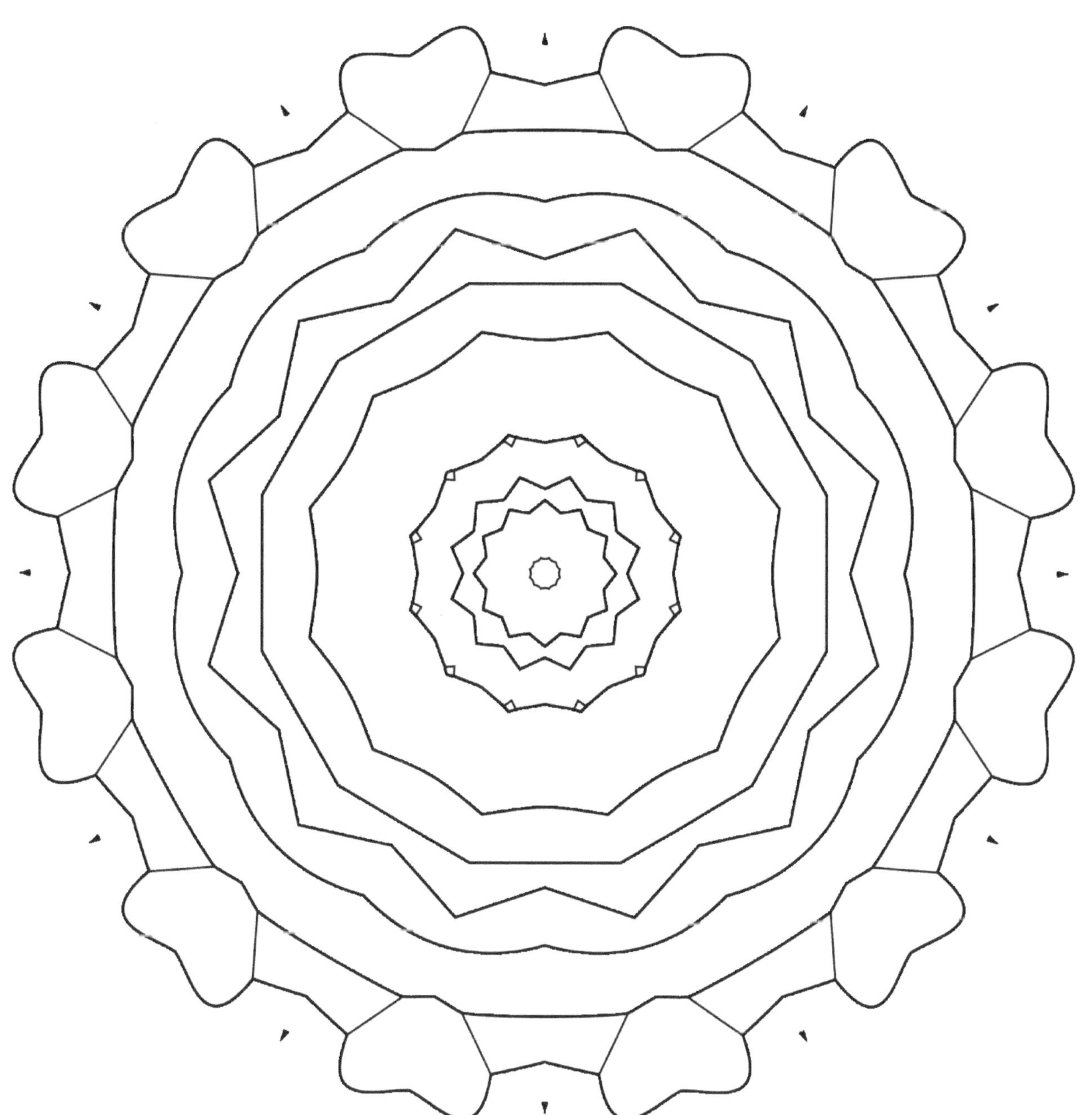

"Fairy tales are more than true: not because they tell us that dragons exist, but because they tell us that dragons can be beaten."

— Neil Gaiman, Coraline

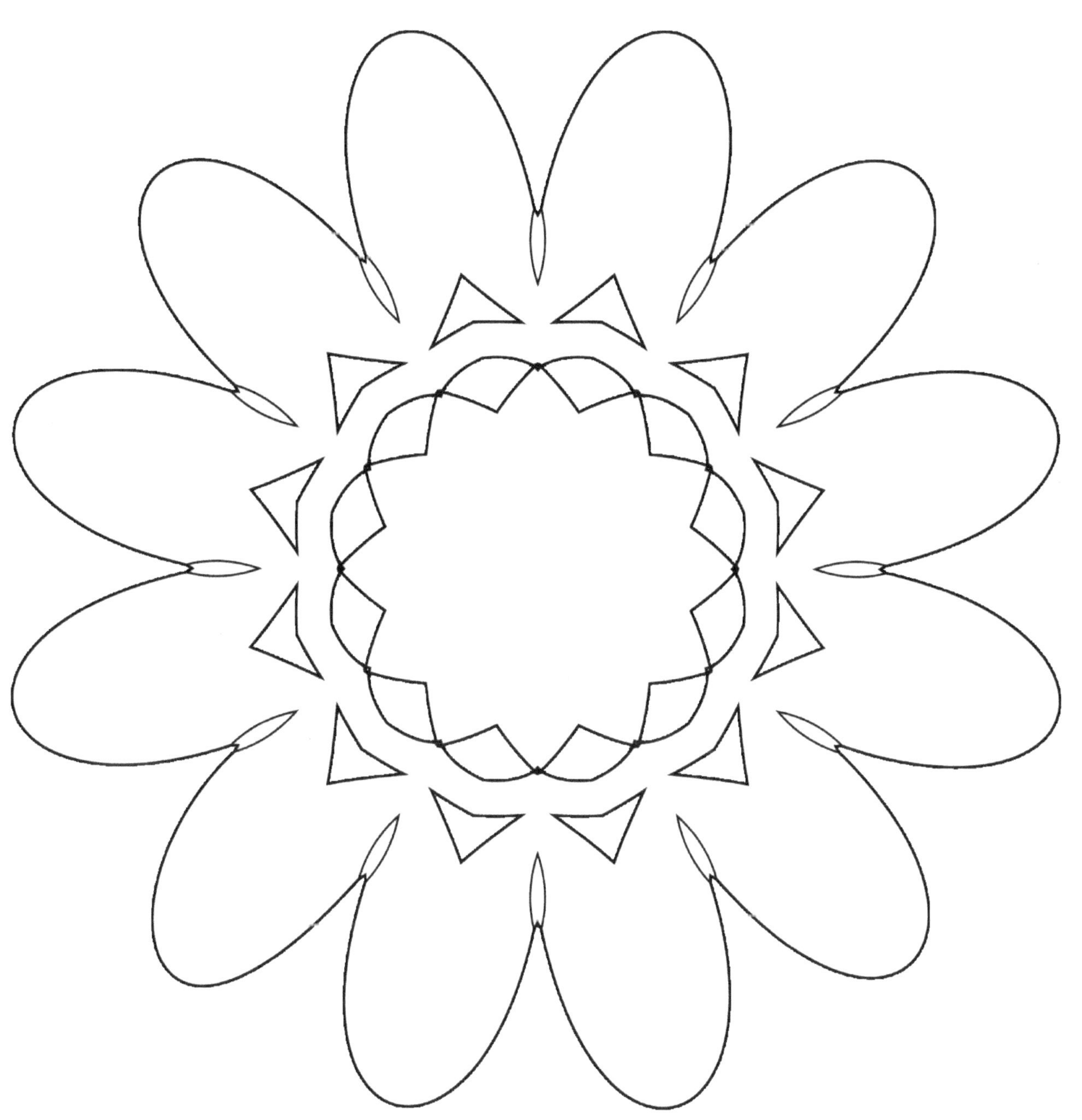

"I am enough of an artist to draw freely upon my imagination. Imagination is more important than knowledge. Knowledge is limited. Imagination encircles the world."

— Albert Einstein

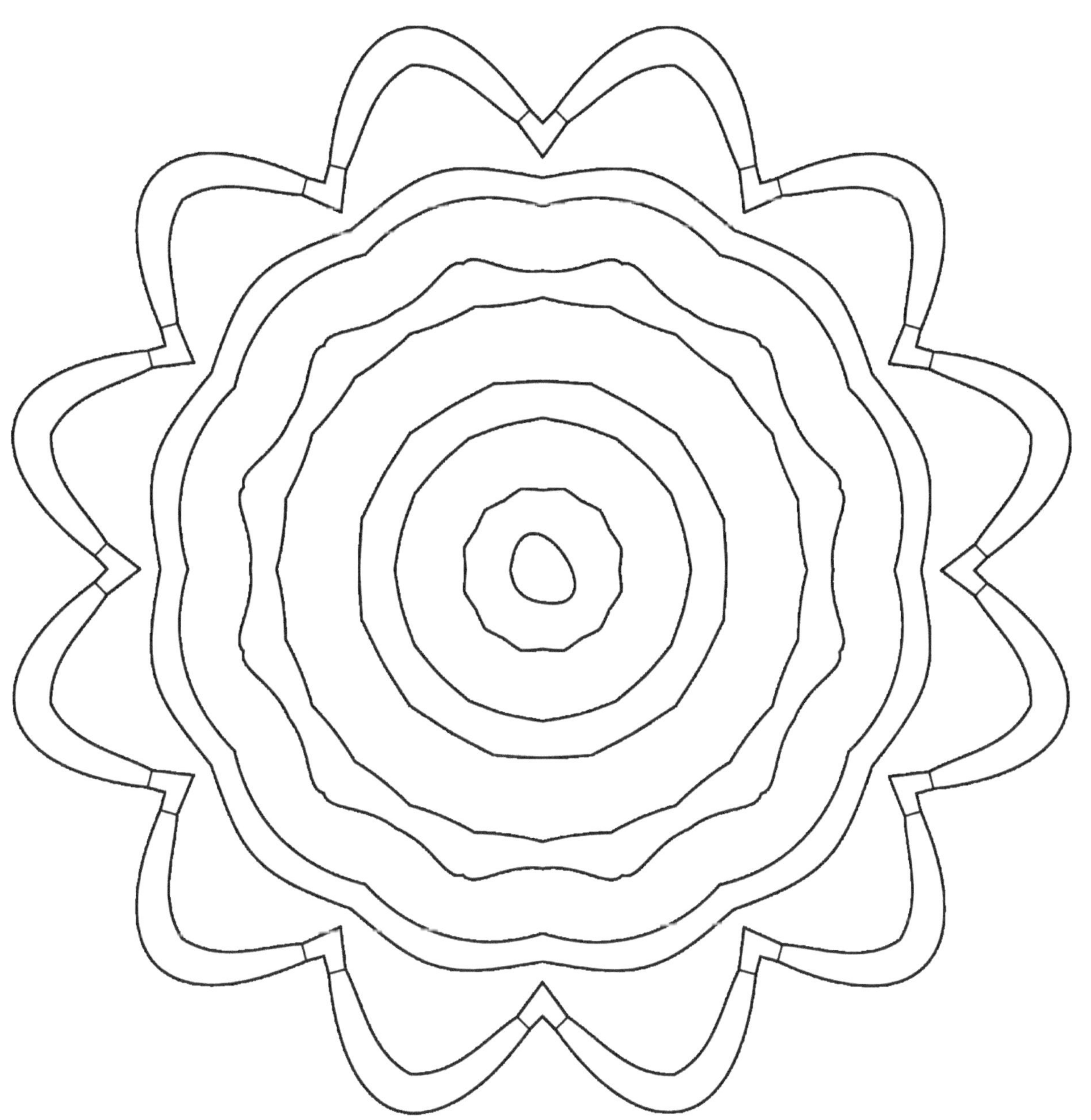

"You have brains in your head. You have feet in your shoes. You can steer yourself any direction you choose. You're on your own. And you know what you know. And YOU are the one who'll decide where to go..."

— Dr. Seuss, Oh, The Places You'll Go!

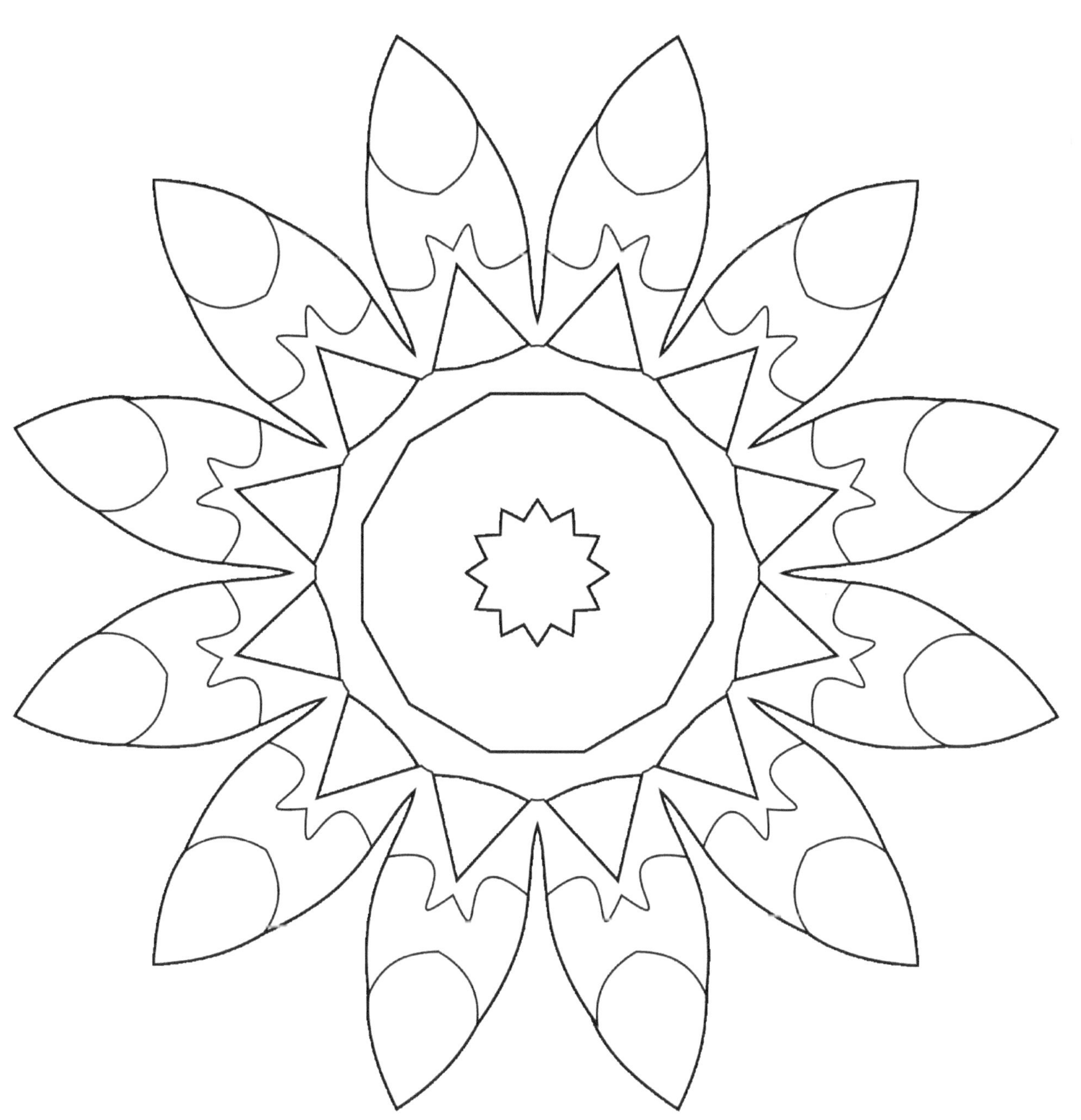

"This life is what you make it. No matter what, you're going to mess up sometimes, it's a universal truth. But the good part is you get to decide how you're going to mess it up. Girls will be your friends - they'll act like it anyway. But just remember, some come, some go. The ones that stay with you through everything - they're your true best friends. Don't let go of them. Also remember, sisters make the best friends in the world. As for lovers, well, they'll come and go too. And baby, I hate to say it, most of them - actually pretty much all of them are going to break your heart, but you can't give up because if you give up, you'll never find your soulmate. You'll never find that half who makes you whole and that goes for everything. Just because you fail once, doesn't mean you're gonna fail at everything. Keep trying, hold on, and always, always, always believe in yourself, because if you don't, then who will, sweetie? So keep your head high, keep your chin up, and most importantly, keep smiling, because life's a beautiful thing and there's so much to smile about."

- Marilyn Monroe

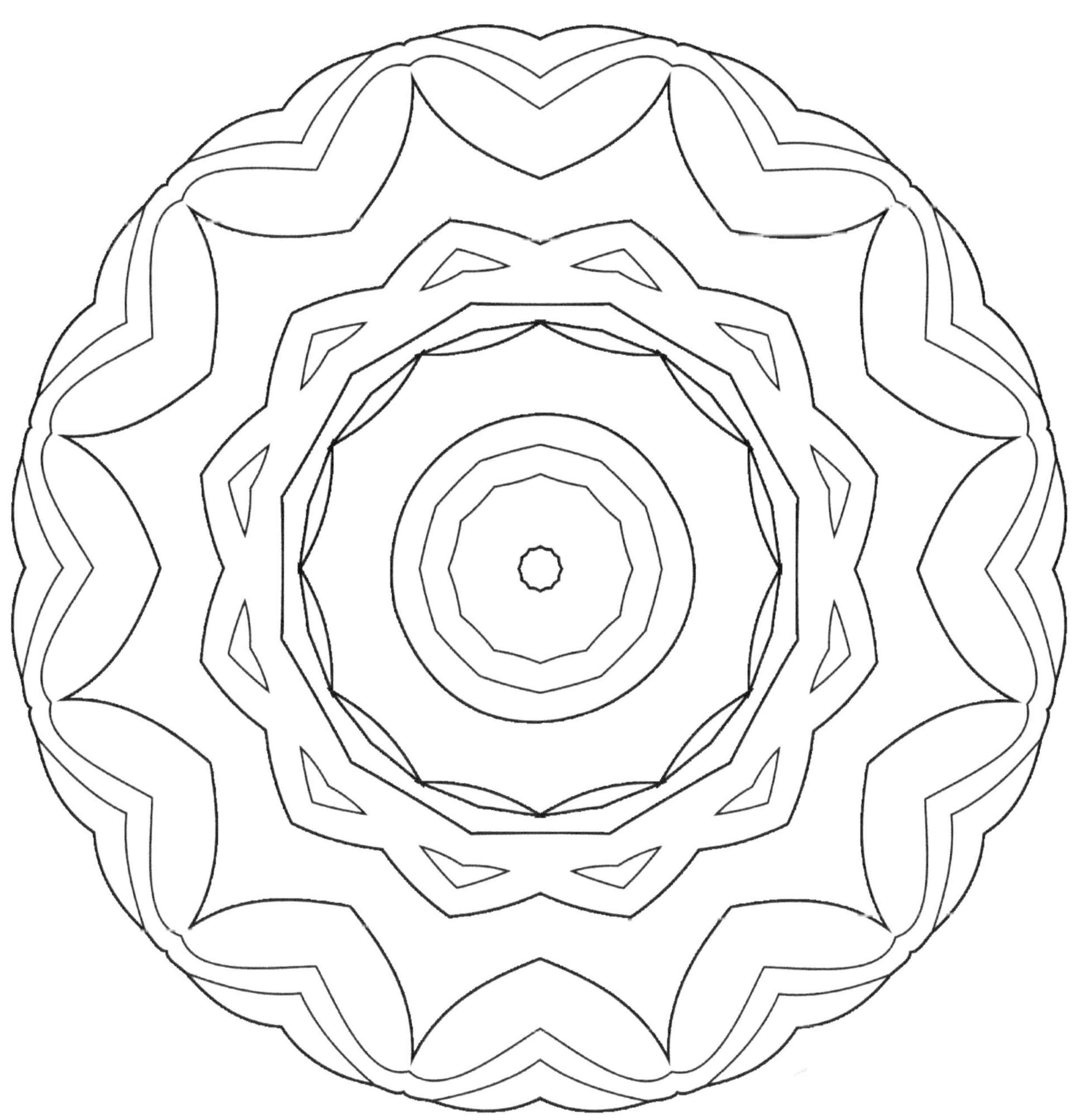

"It is never too late to be what you might have been."

— George Eliot

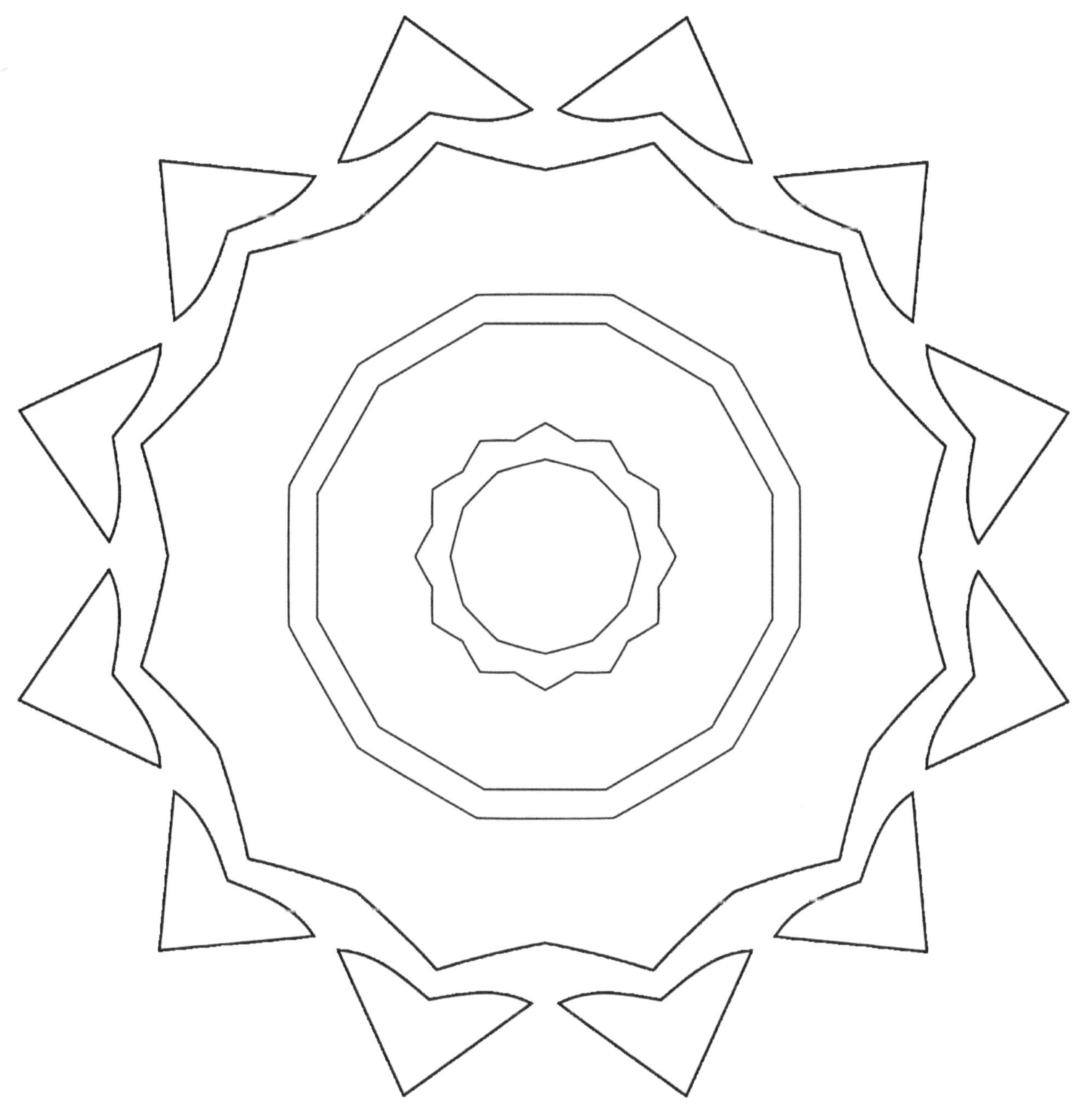

"Everything you can imagine is real."

— Pablo Picasso

"There is no greater agony than bearing an untold story inside you."

— Maya Angelou, I Know Why the Caged Bird Sings

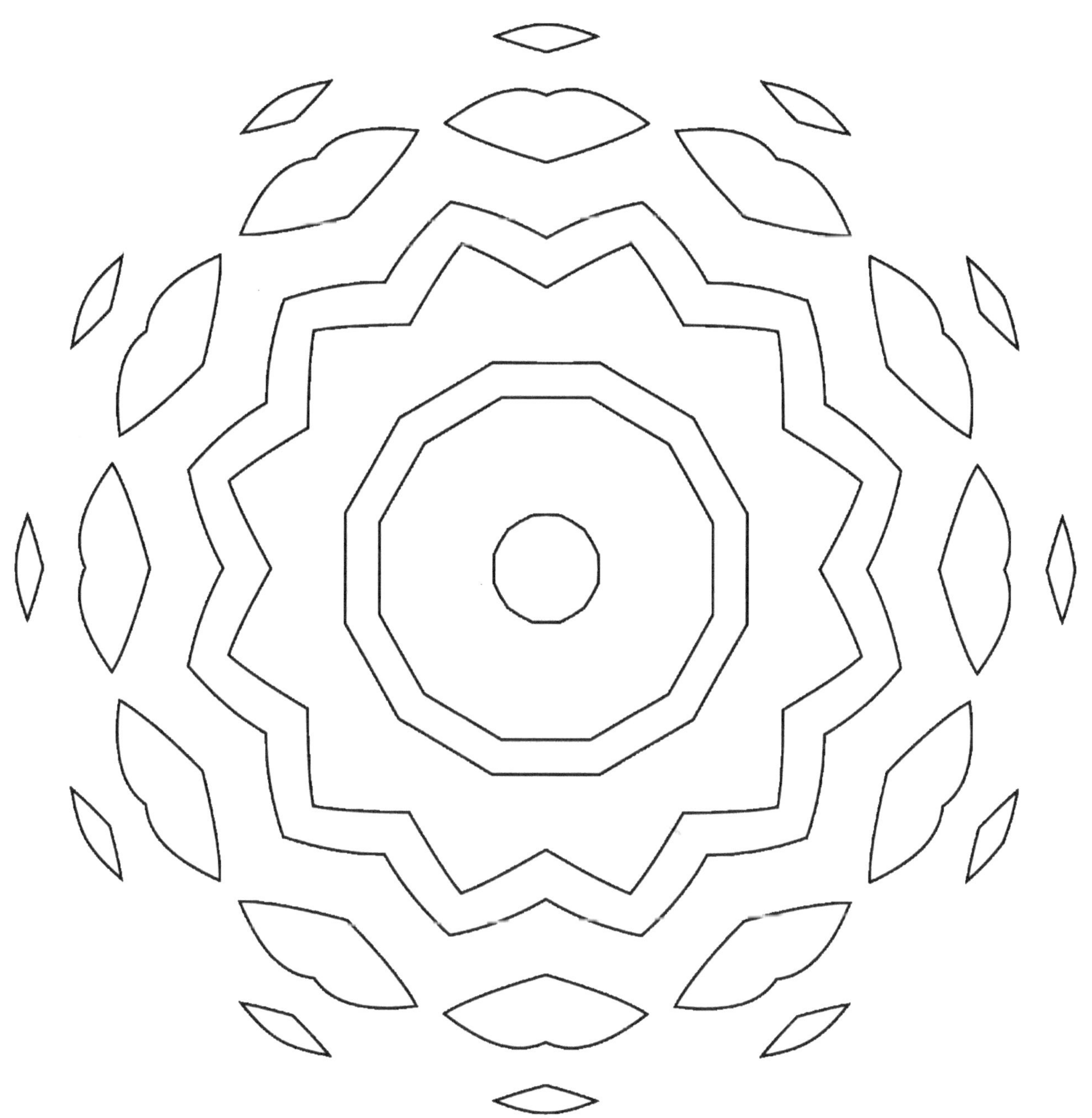

"Do what you can,
with what you have,
where you are."

— Theodore Roosevelt

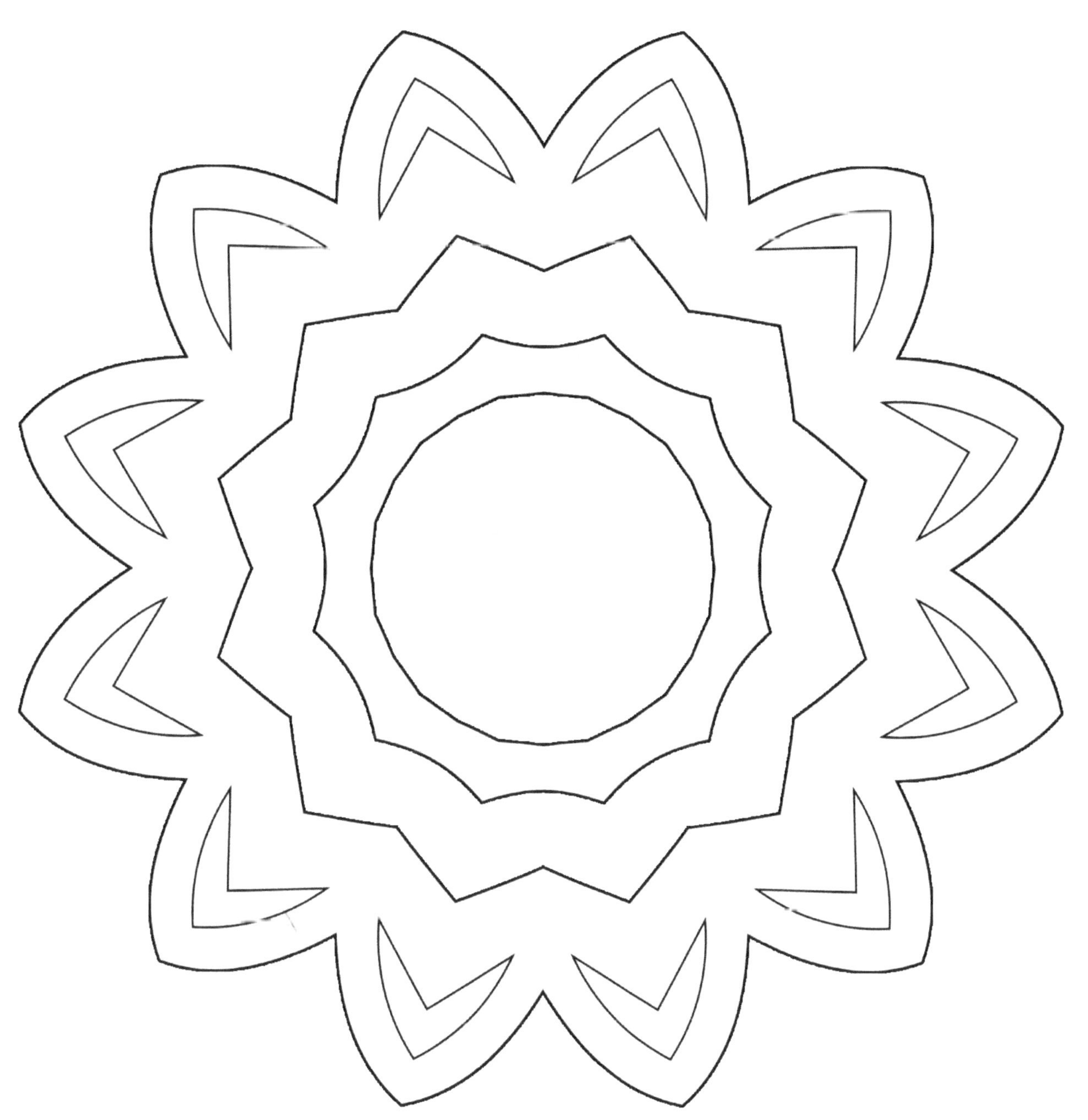

"You can never get a
cup of tea large
enough or a book long
enough to suit me."

— C.S. Lewis

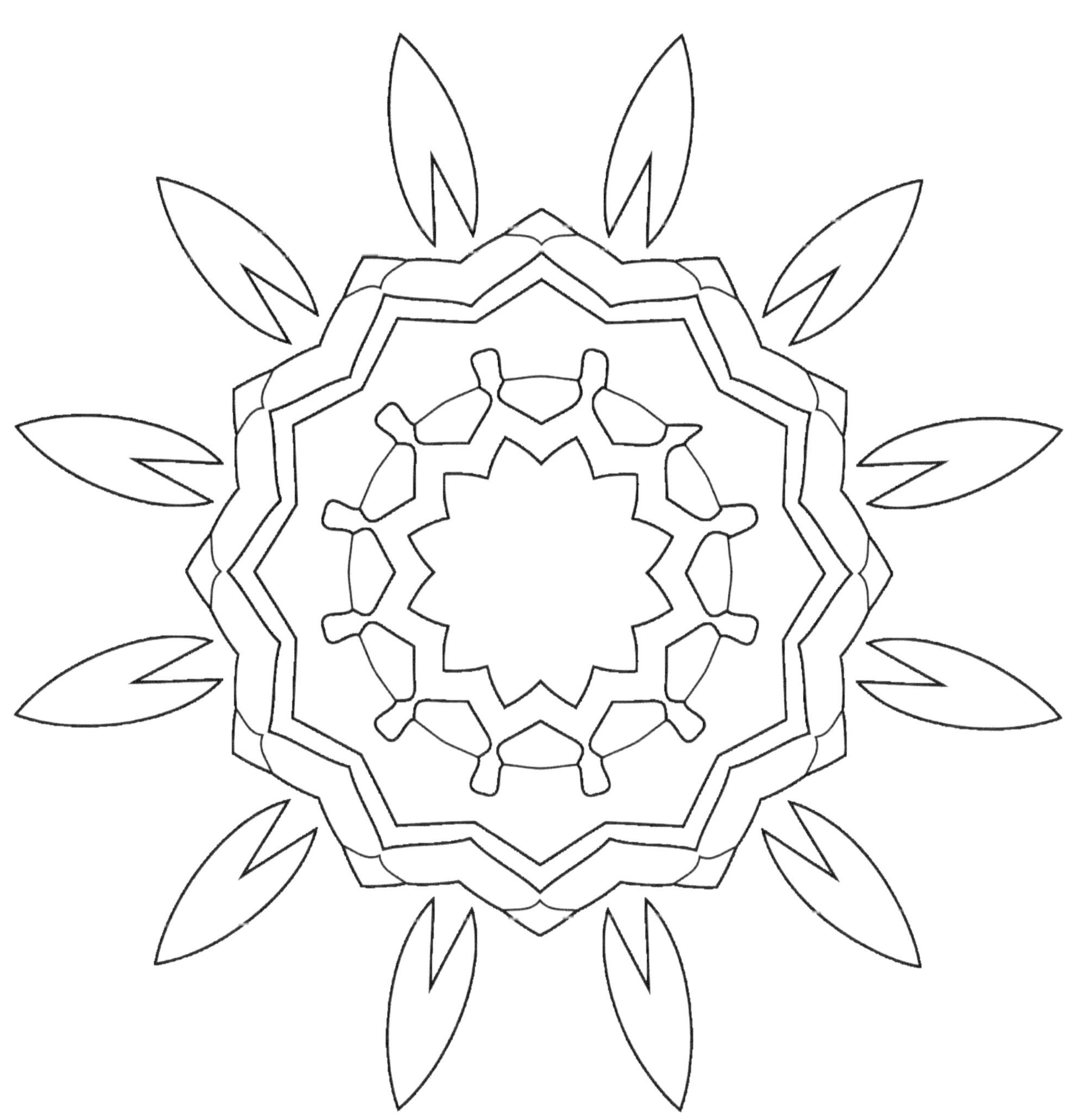

"Listen to the mustn'ts, child. Listen to the don'ts. Listen to the shouldn'ts, the impossibles, the won'ts. Listen to the never haves, then listen close to me... Anything can happen, child. Anything can be."

— Shel Silverstein

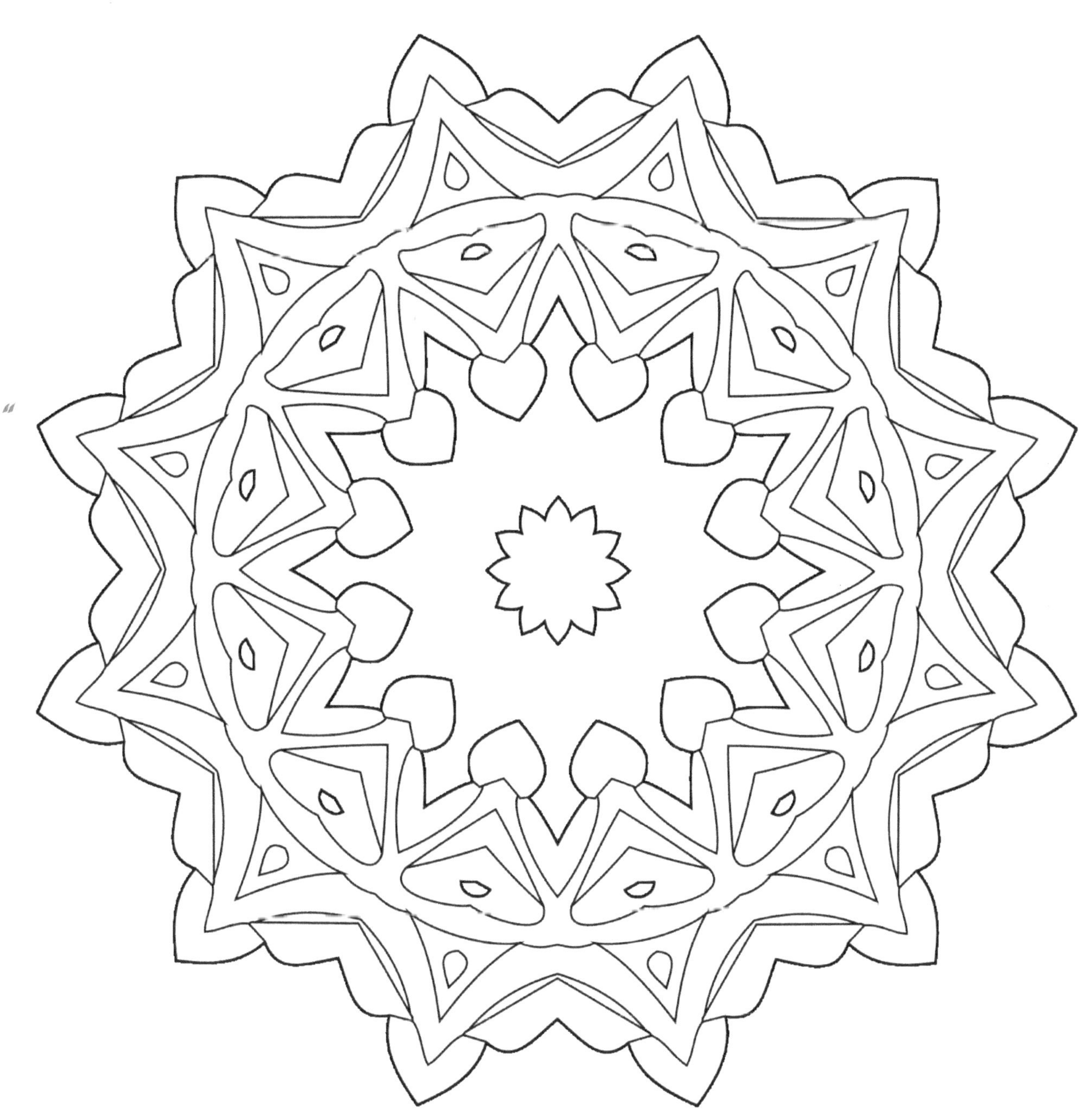

"To the well-organized mind, death is but the next great adventure."

— J.K. Rowling, Harry Potter and the Sorcerer's Stone

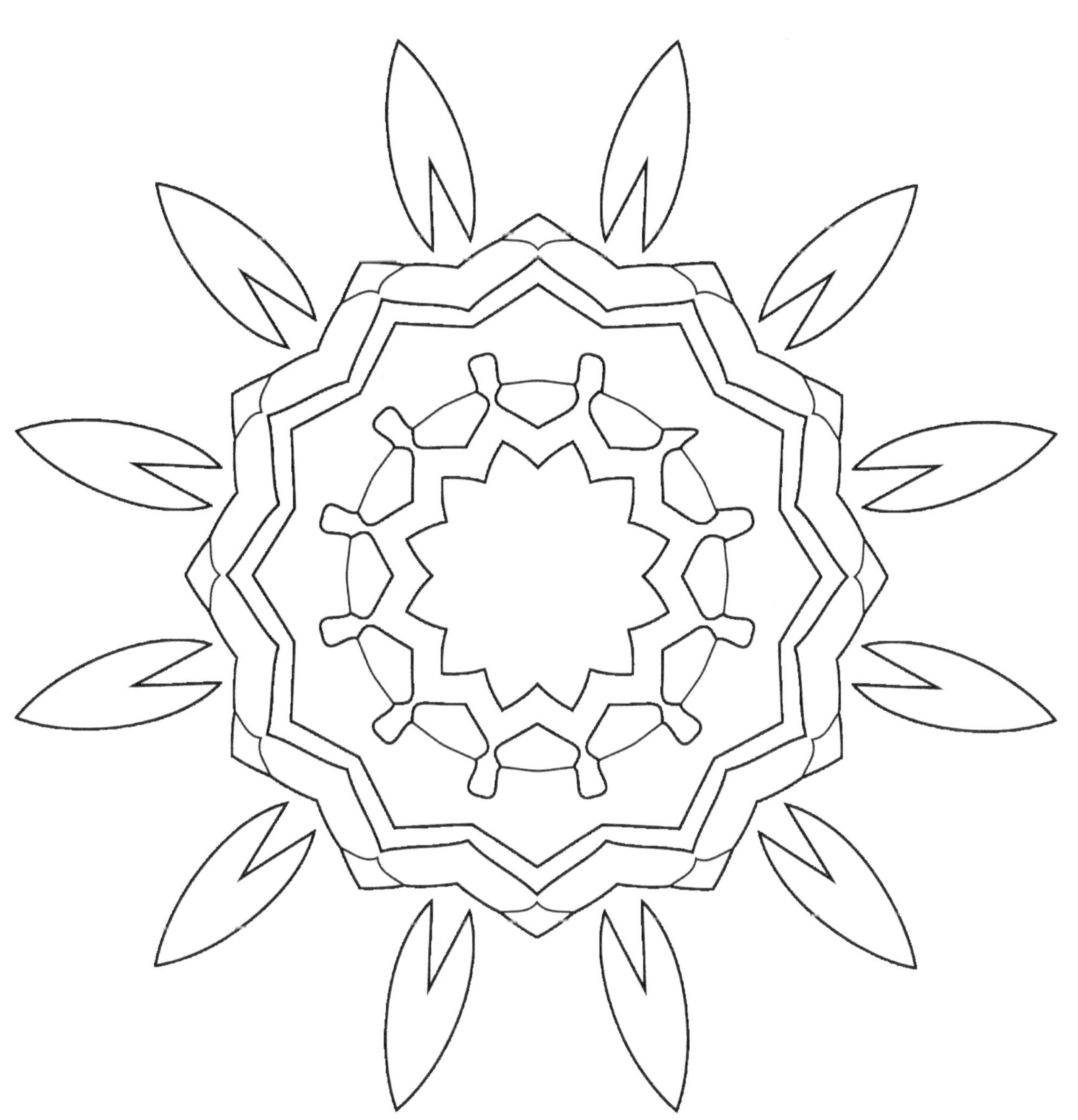

"Listen to the mustn'ts, child. Listen to the don'ts. Listen to the shouldn'ts, the impossibles, the won'ts. Listen to the never haves, then listen close to me... Anything can happen, child. Anything can be."

— Shel Silverstein

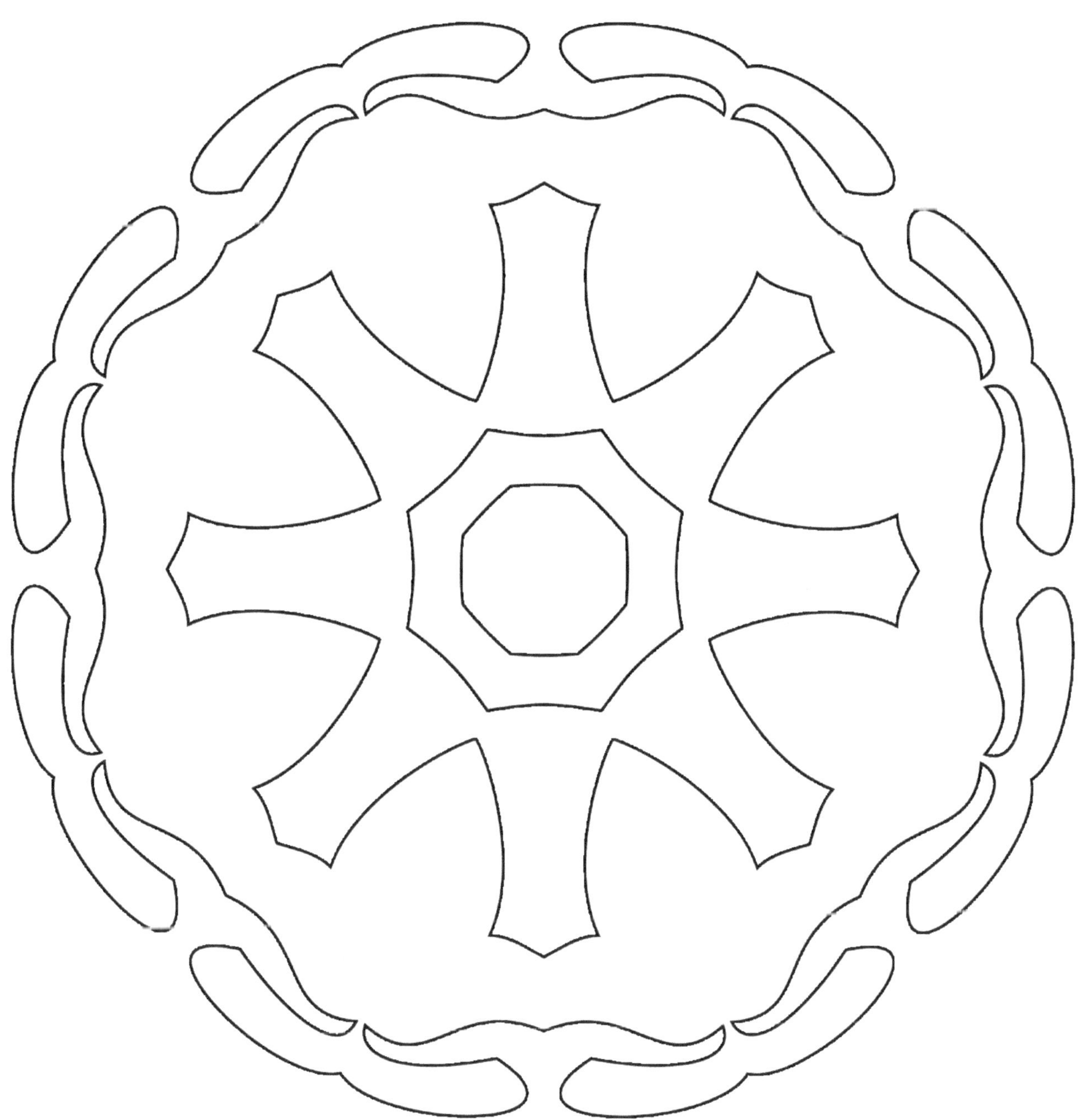

"To the well-organized mind, death is but the next great adventure."

— J.K. Rowling, Harry Potter and the Sorcerer's Stone

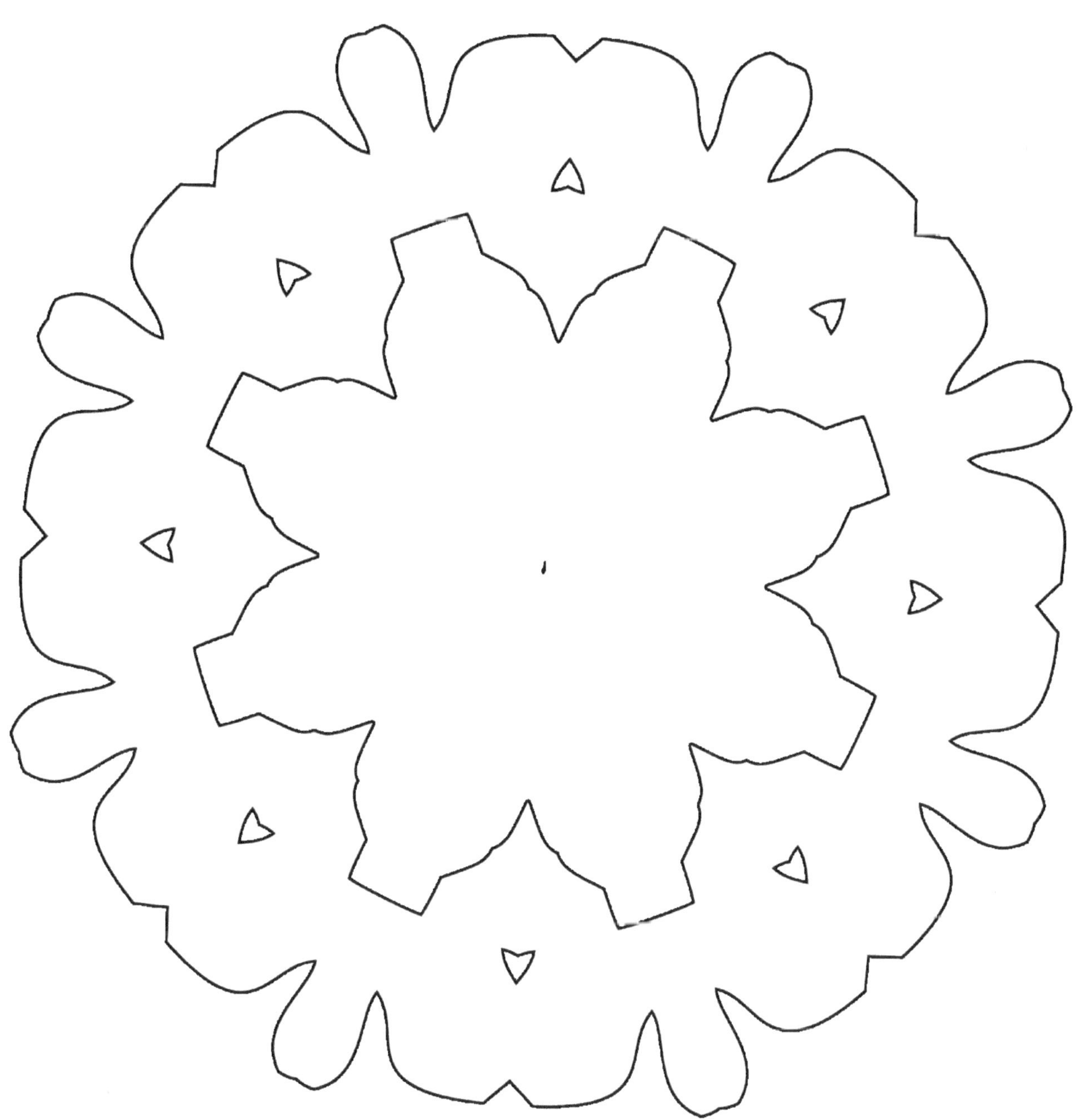

"When one door of
happiness closes,
another opens; but
often we look so
long at the closed
door that we do
not see the one
which has been
opened for us."

— Helen Keller

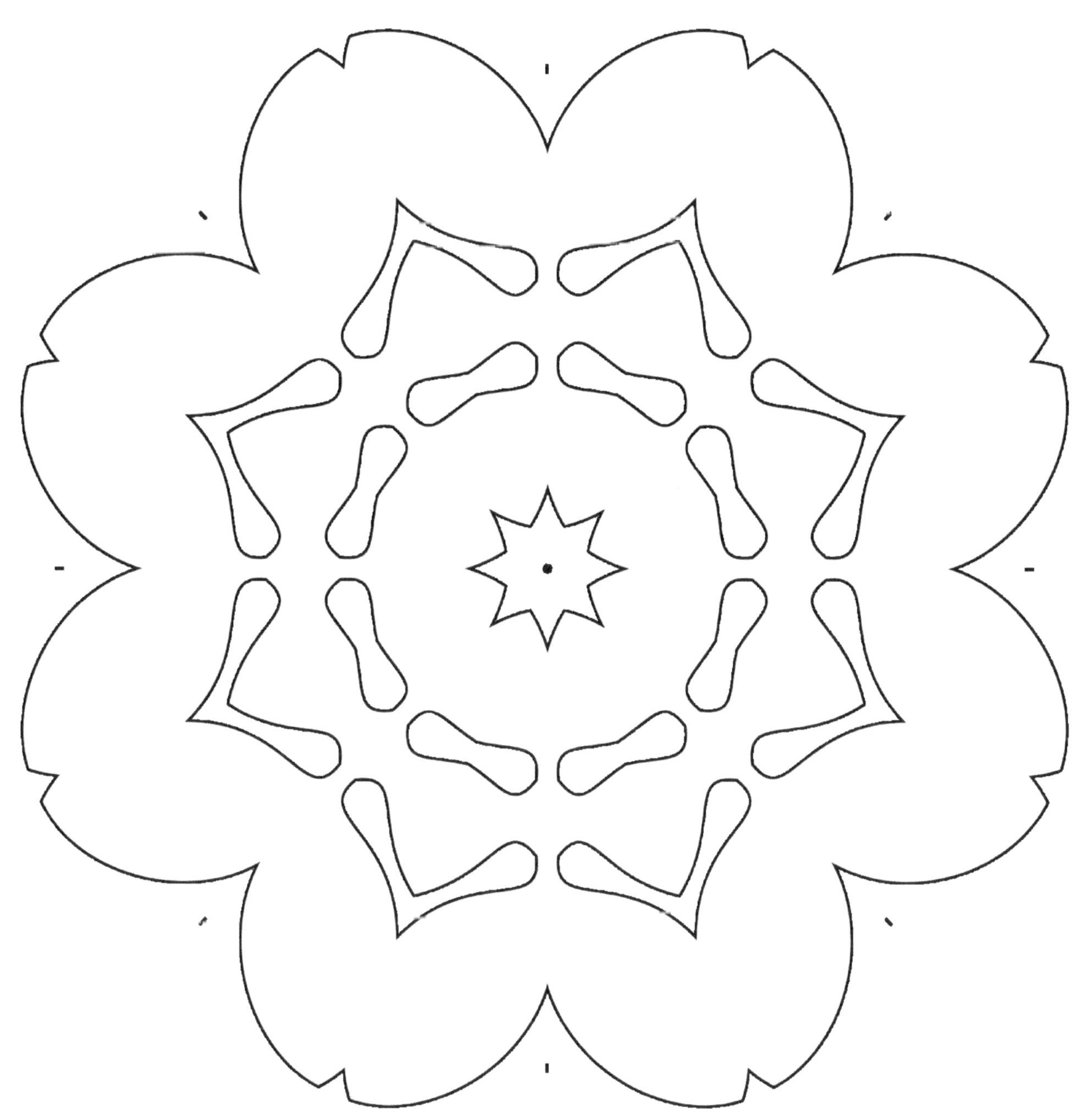

"Life isn't about
finding yourself.
Life is about
creating yourself."

— George Bernard Shaw

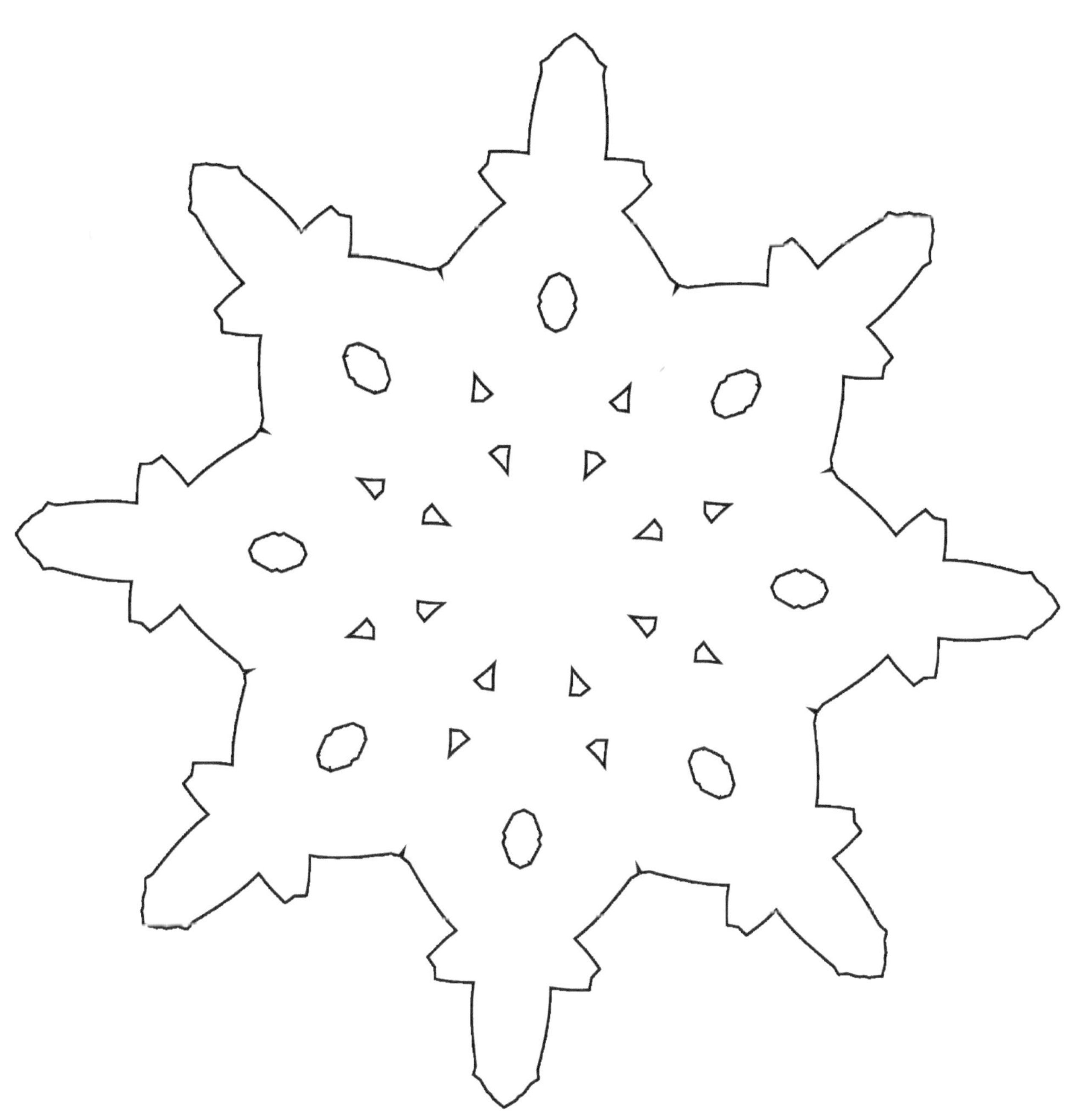

"Success is not
Final, Failure is not
Fatal: it is the
courage to continue
that counts."

— Winston S. Churchill

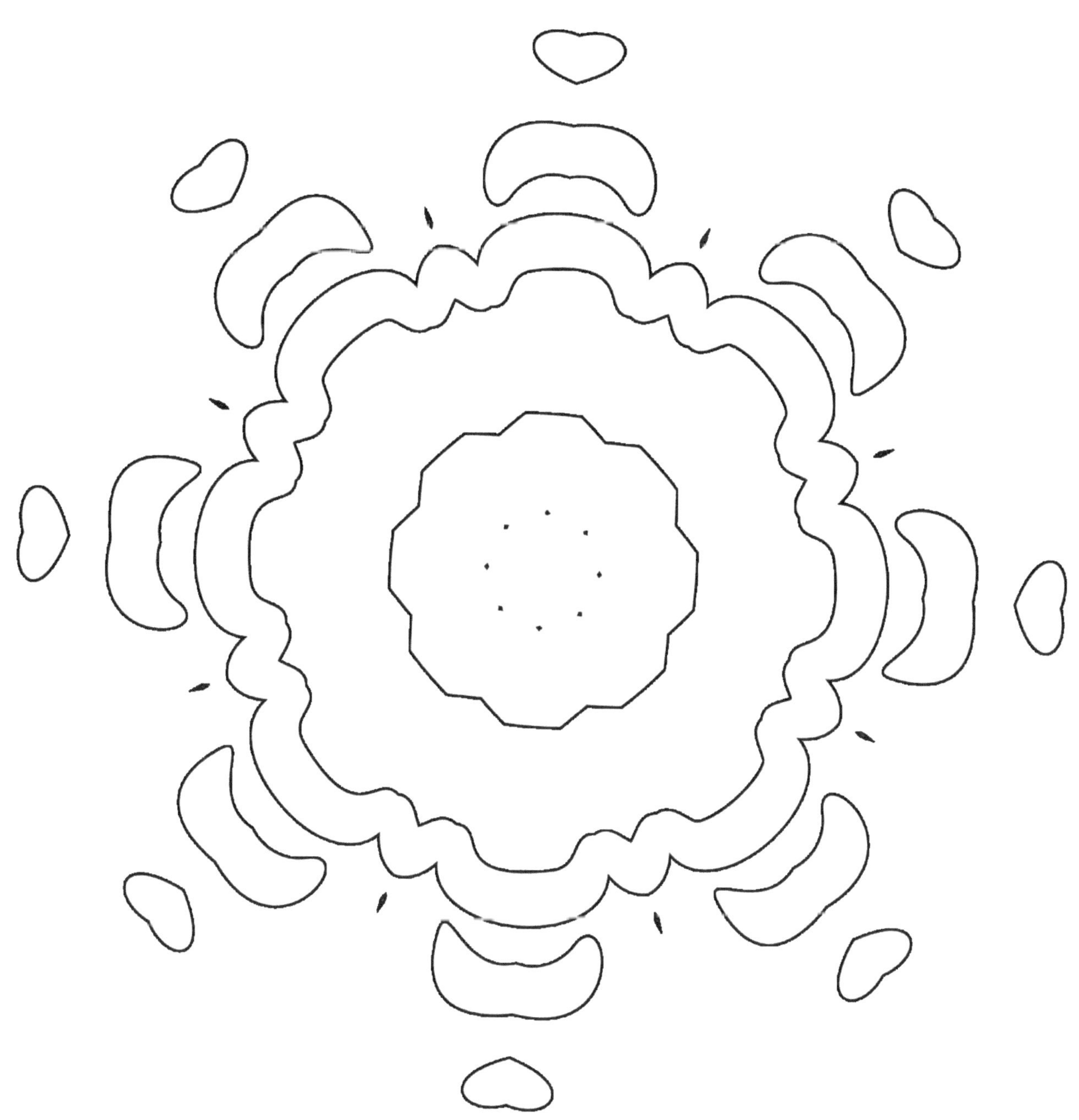

"I believe in manicures. I believe in overdressing. I believe in primping at leisure and wearing lipstick. I believe in pink. I believe that loving is the best calorie-burner. I believe in kissing. I believe that happy girls are the prettiest girls... and I believe in miracles."

— Unknown

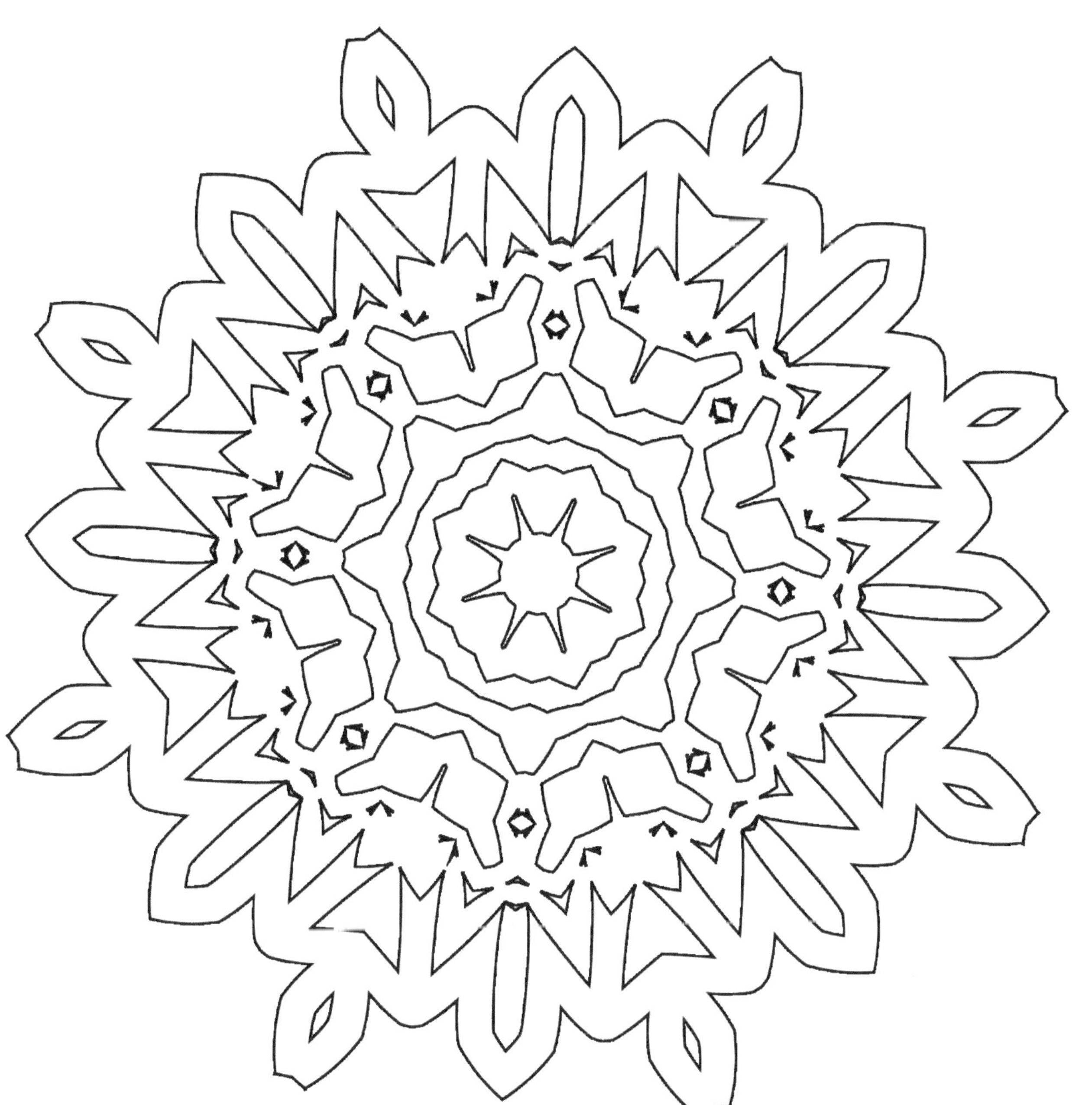

"So, this is my life. And I want you to know that I am both happy and sad and I'm still trying to figure out how that could be."

— Stephen Chbosky, The Perks of Being a Wallflower

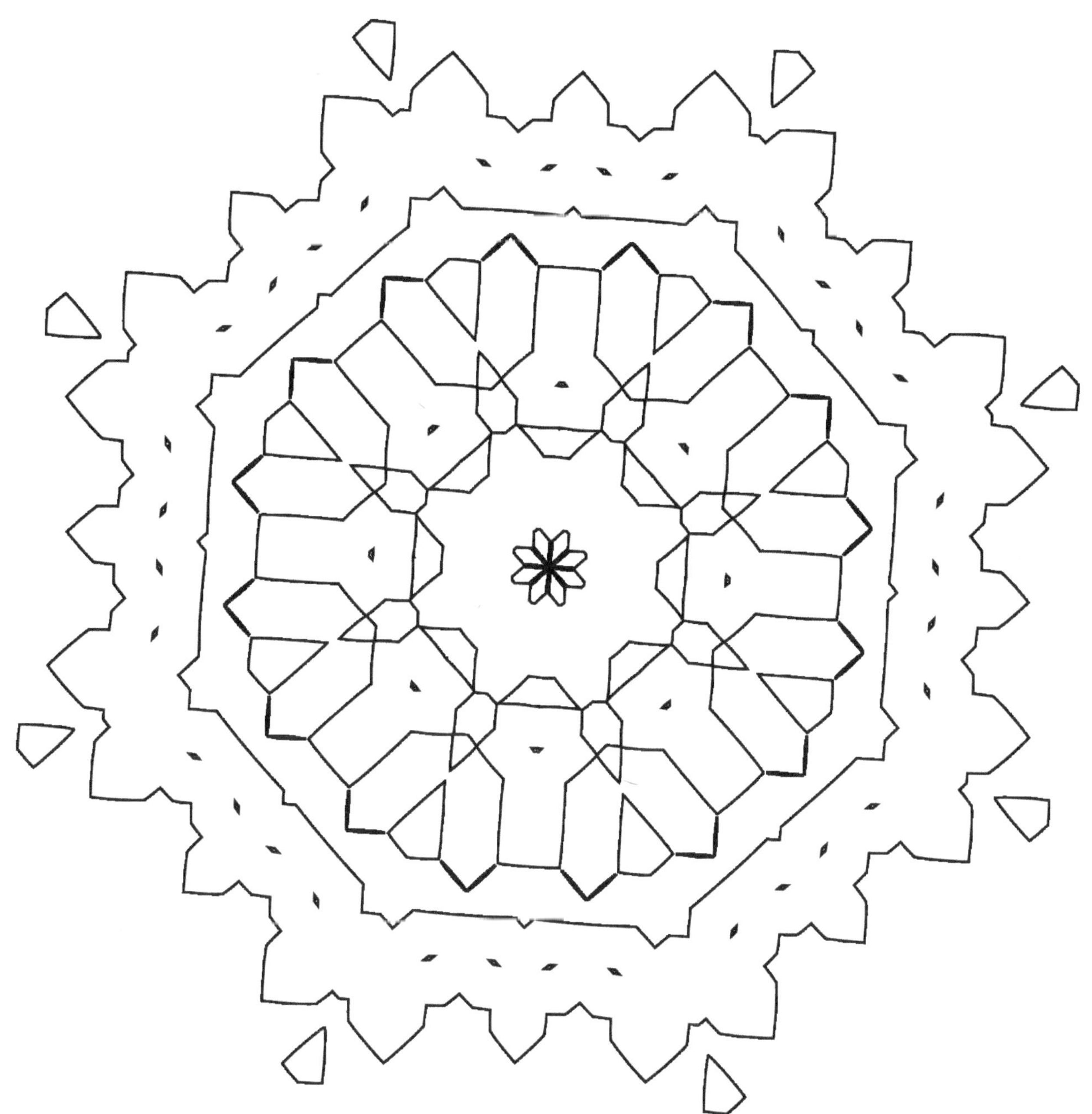

"You may say I'm a dreamer, but I'm not the only one. I hope someday you'll join us. And the world will live as one."

— John Lennon

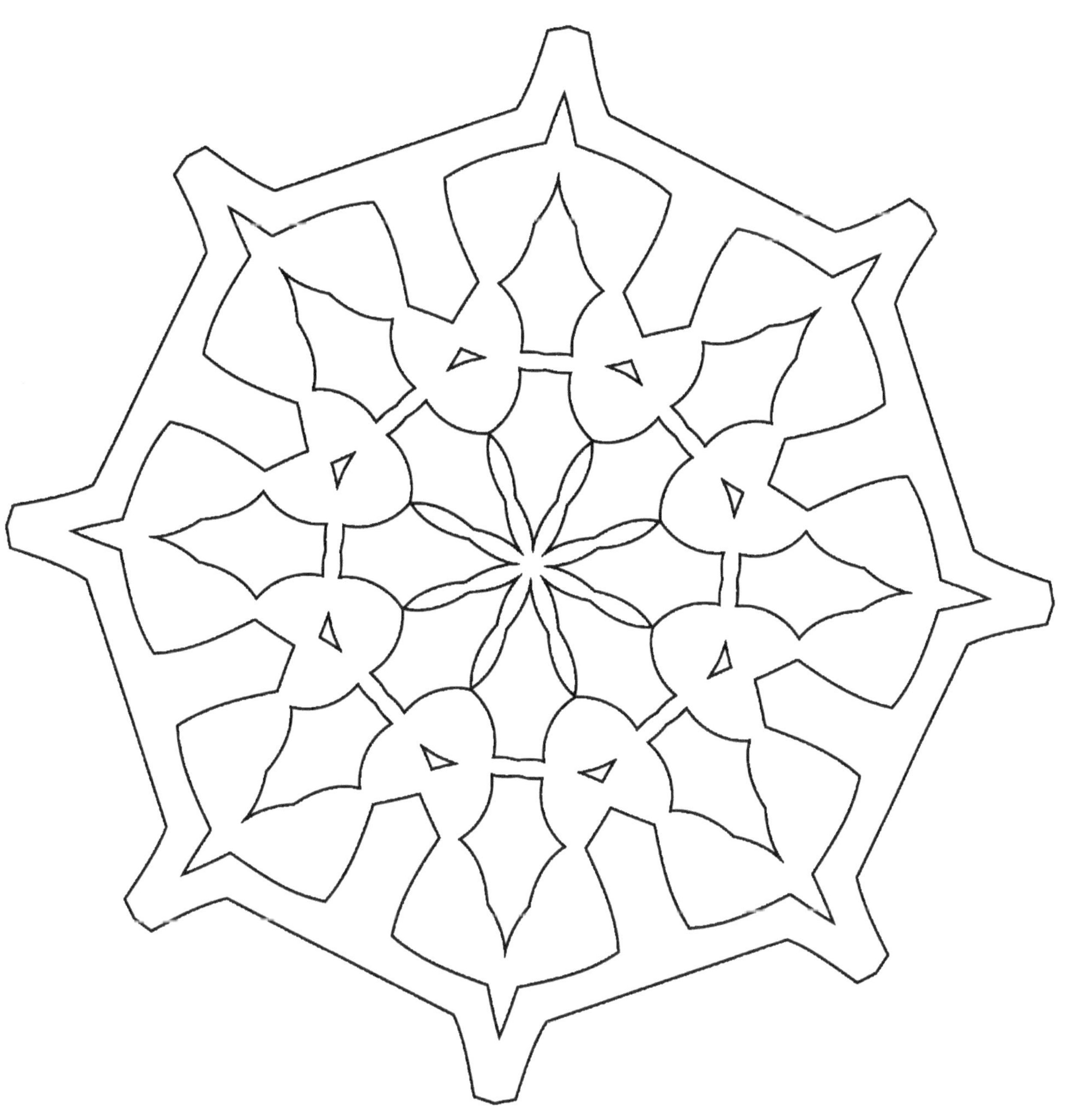

"Our deepest fear is not that we are inadequate. Our deepest fear is that we are powerful beyond measure. It is our light, not our darkness that most frightens us. We ask ourselves, 'Who am I to be brilliant, gorgeous, talented, fabulous?' Actually, who are you not to be? You are a child of God. Your playing small does not serve the world. There is nothing enlightened about shrinking so that other people won't feel insecure around you. We are all meant to shine, as children do. We were born to make manifest the glory of God that is within us. It's not just in some of us; it's in everyone. And as we let our own light shine, we unconsciously give other people permission to do the same. As we are liberated from our own fear, our presence automatically liberates others."

- — Marianne Williamson, A Return to Love: Reflections on the Principles of "A Course in Miracles"

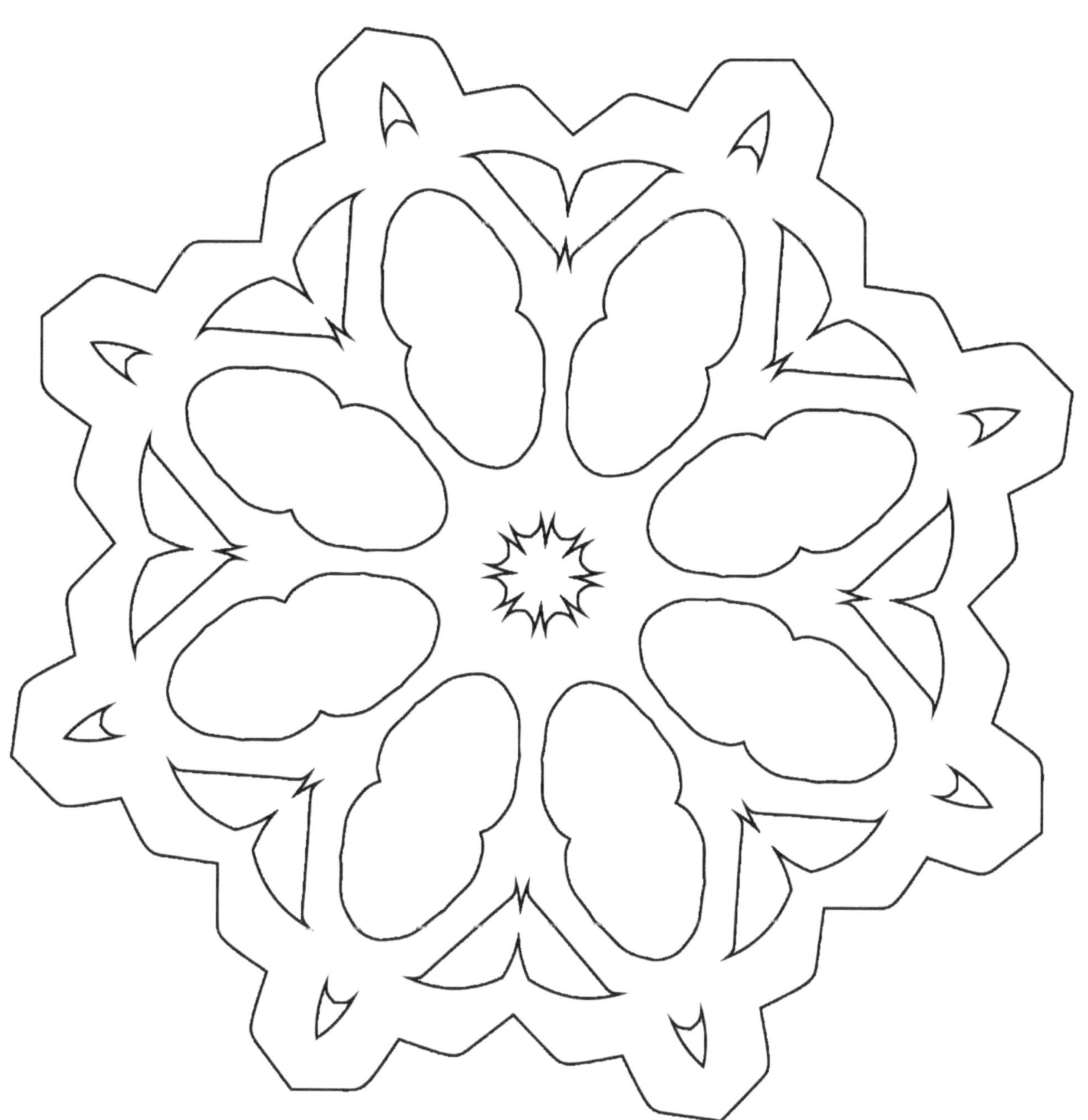

"And, when you want something, all the universe conspires in helping you to achieve it."

— Paulo Coelho, The Alchemist

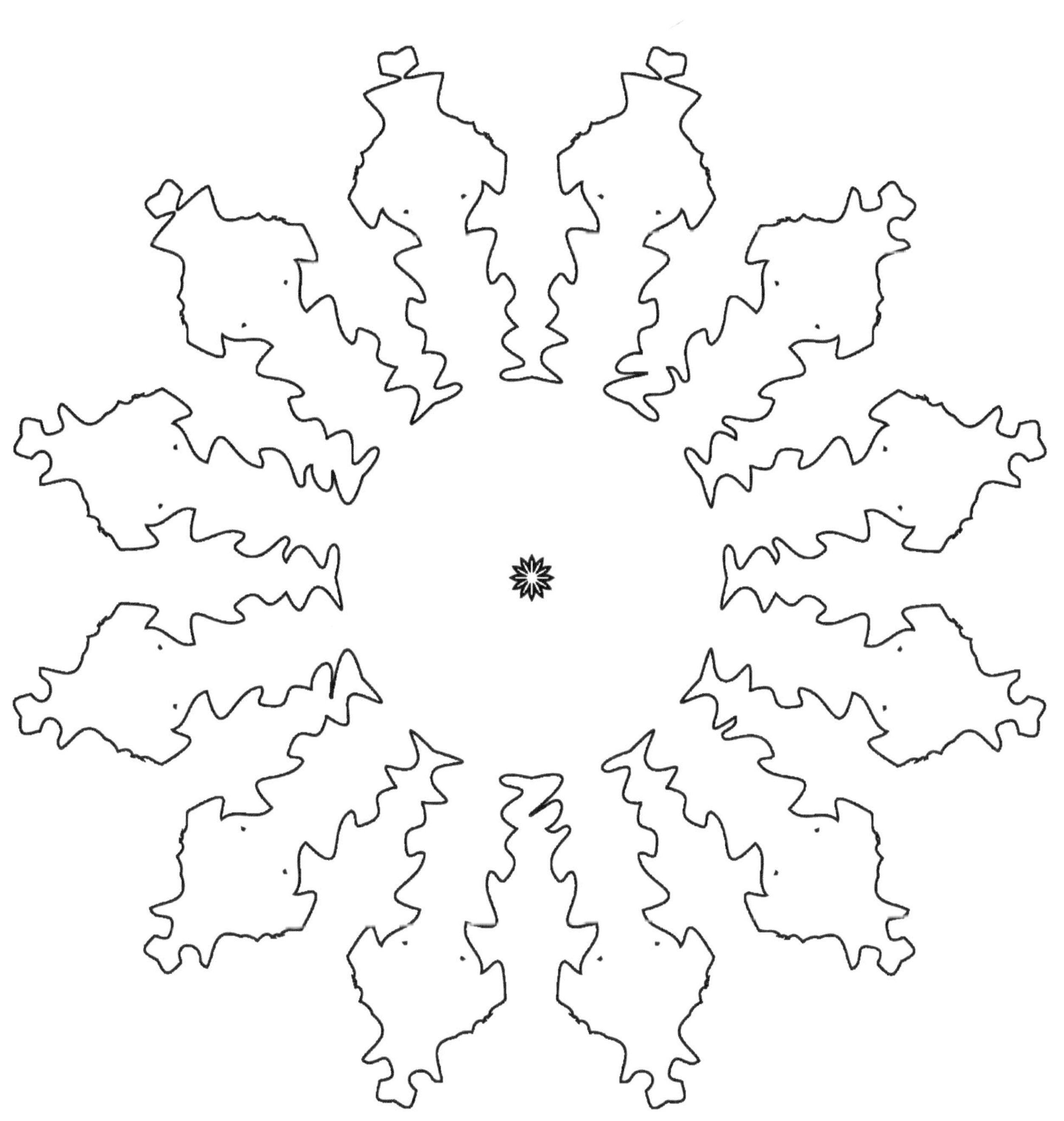

"A person's a person, no matter how small."

— Dr. Seuss, Horton Hears a Who!

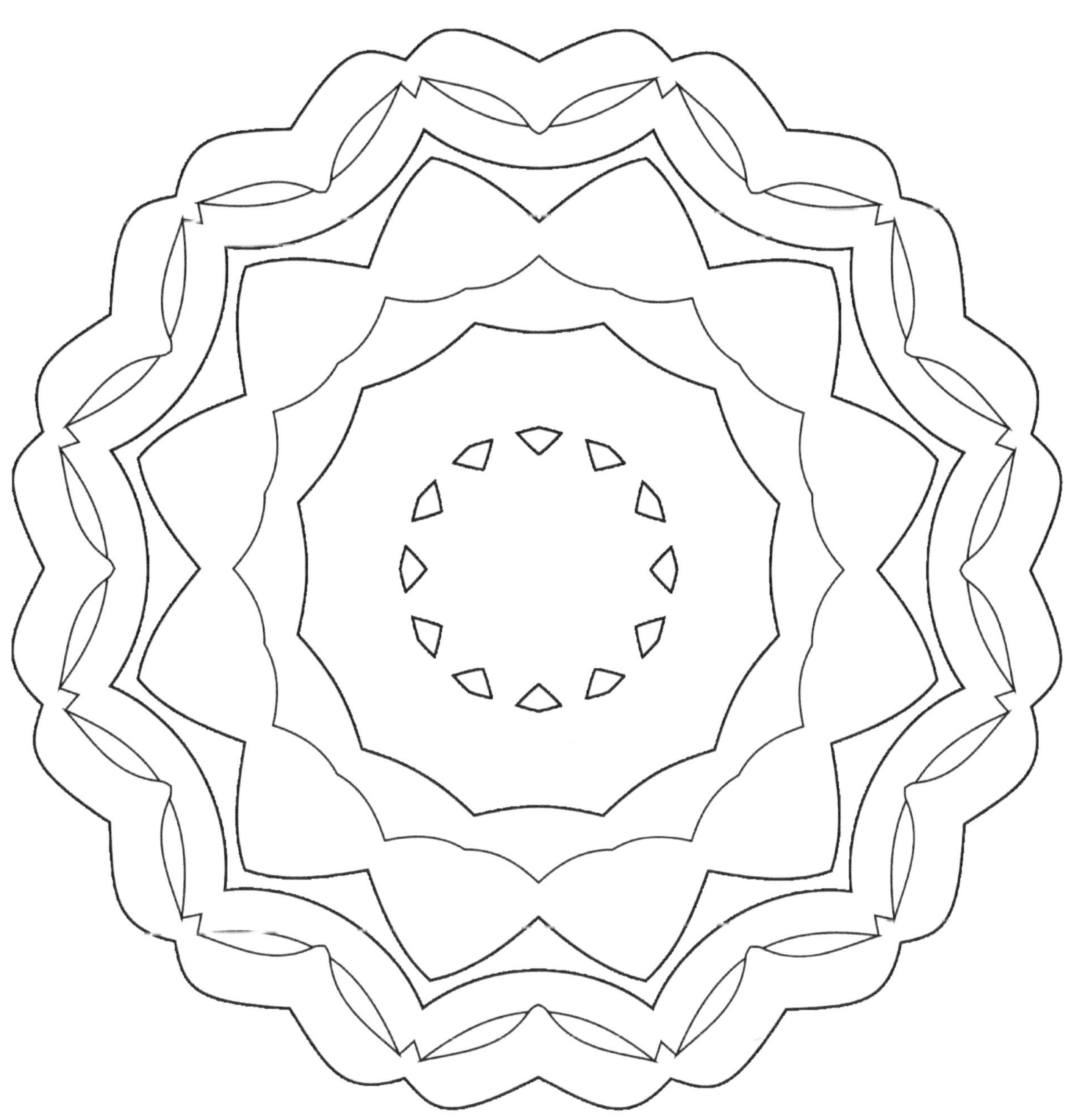

"What you're supposed to do when you don't like a thing is change it. If you can't change it, change the way you think about it. Don't complain."

— Maya Angelou, Wouldn't Take Nothing for My Journey Now

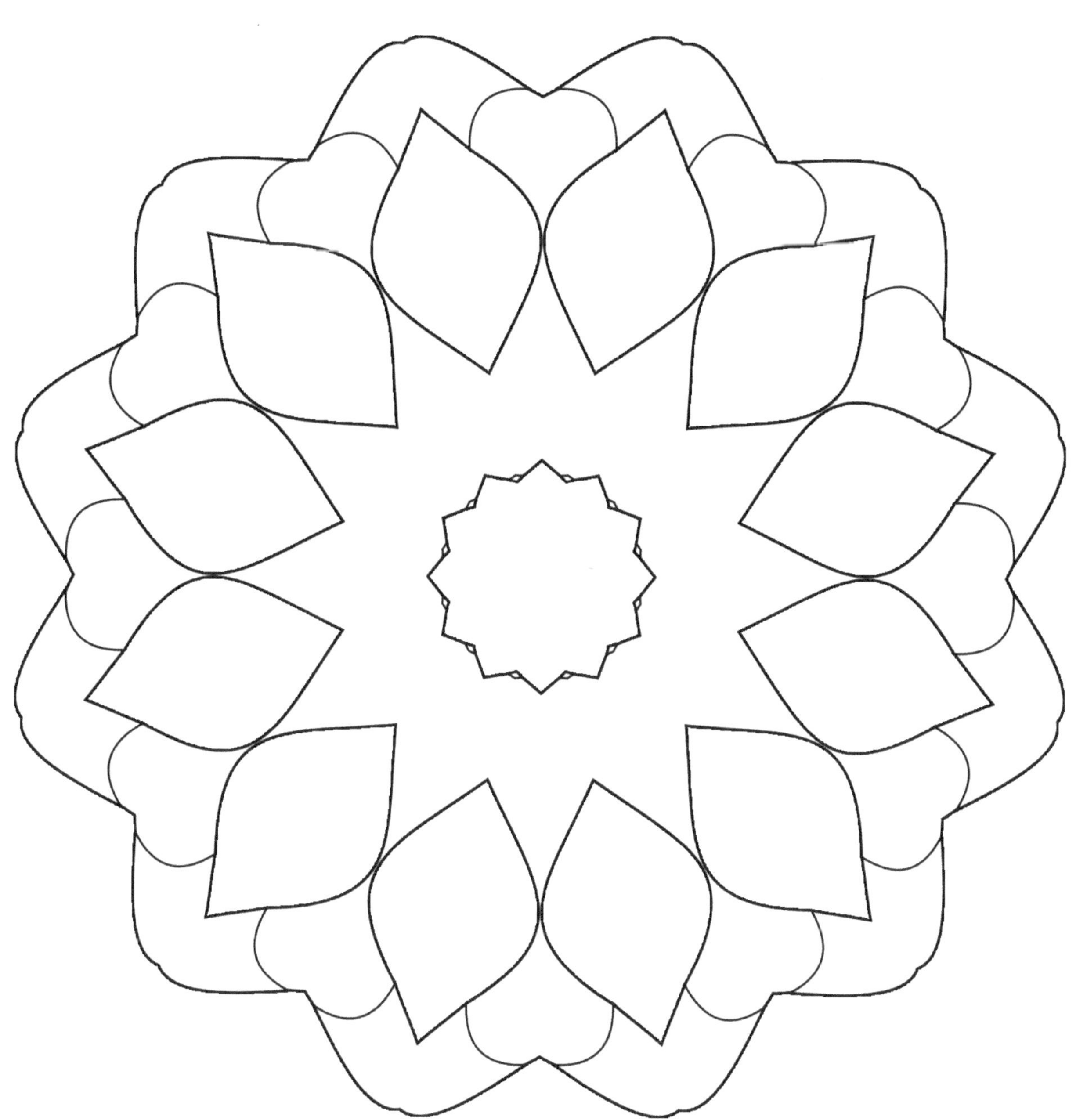

"It's no use going back to yesterday, because I was a different person then."

— Lewis Carroll, Alice in Wonderland

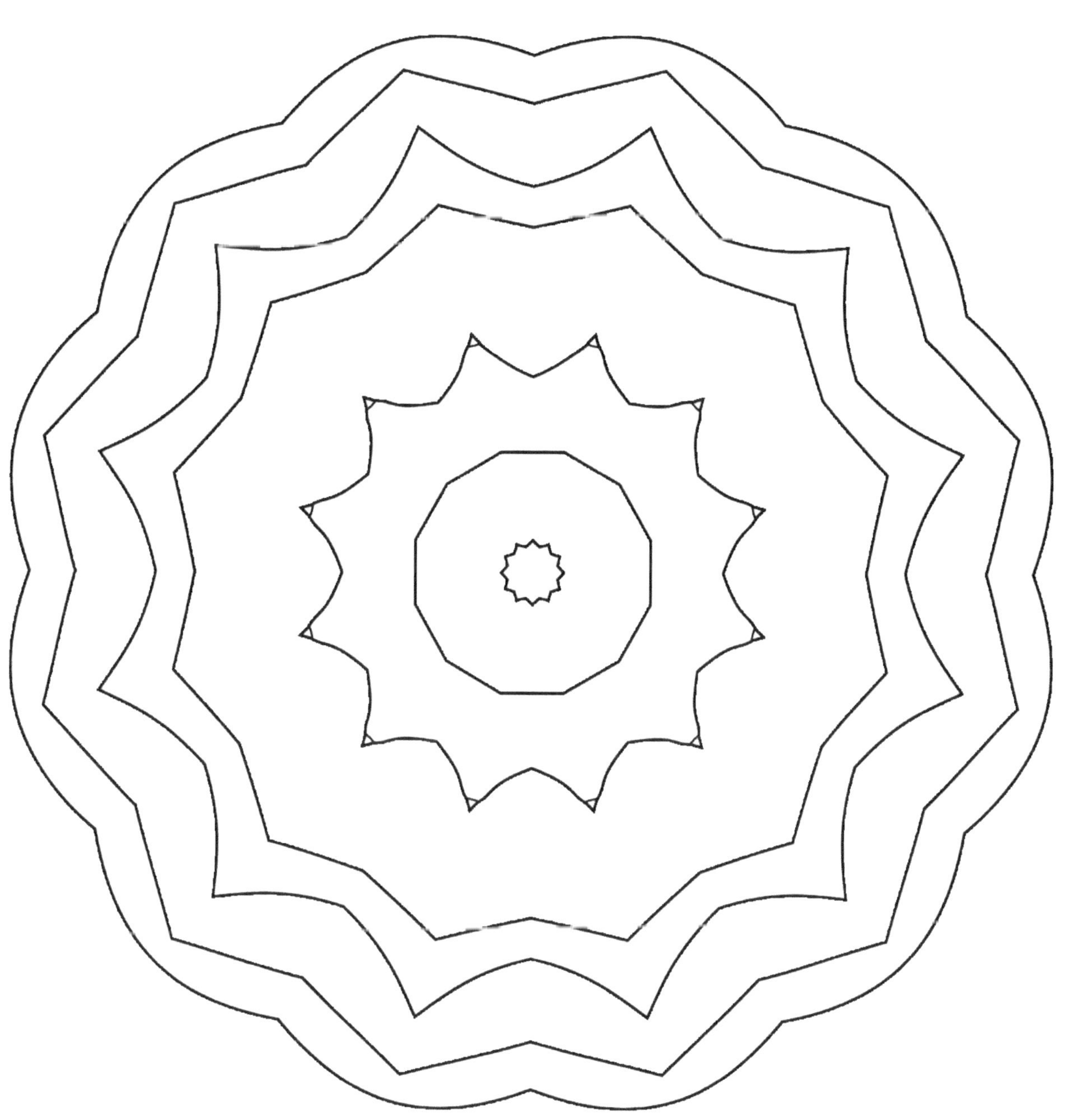

You can't live your life for other people. You've got to do what's right for you, even if it hurts some people you love."

— Nicholas Sparks, The Notebook

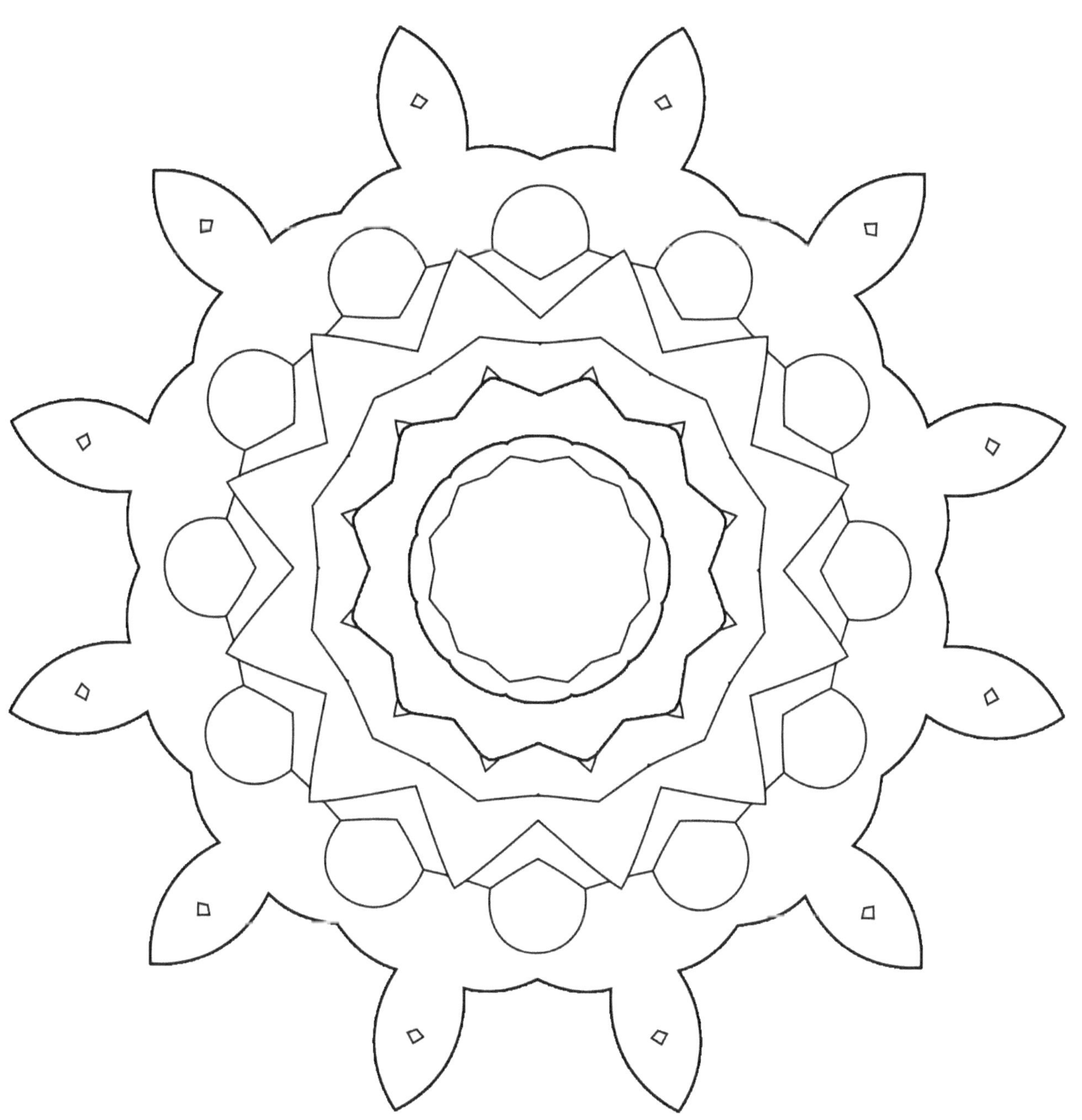

"He's not perfect. You aren't either, and the two of you will never be perfect. But if he can make you laugh at least once, causes you to think twice, and if he admits to being human and making mistakes, hold onto him and give him the most you can. He isn't going to quote poetry, he's not thinking about you every moment, but he will give you a part of him that he knows you could break. Don't hurt him, don't change him, and don't expect for more than he can give. Don't analyze. Smile when he makes you happy, yell when he makes you mad, and miss him when he's not there. Love hard when there is love to be had. Because perfect guys don't exist, but there's always one guy that is perfect for you."

— Bob Marley

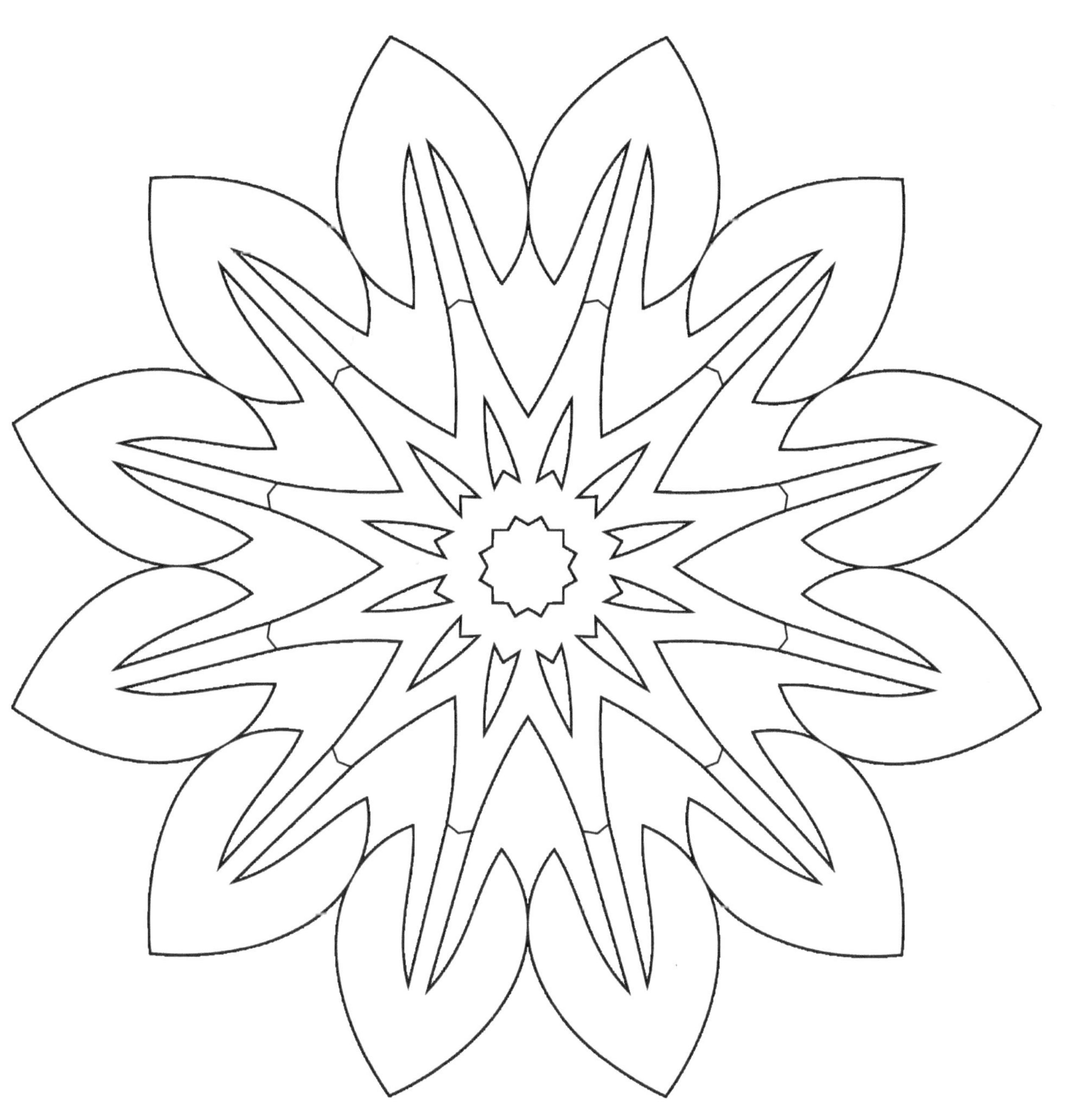

"When we honestly ask ourselves which person in our lives mean the most to us, we often find that it is those who, instead of giving advice, solutions, or cures, have chosen rather to share our pain and touch our wounds with a warm and tender hand. The friend who can be silent with us in a moment of despair or confusion, who can stay with us in an hour of grief and bereavement, who can tolerate not knowing, not curing, not healing and face with us the reality of our powerlessness, that is a friend who cares."

— Henri J.M. Nouwen, Out of Solitude: Three Meditations on the Christian Life

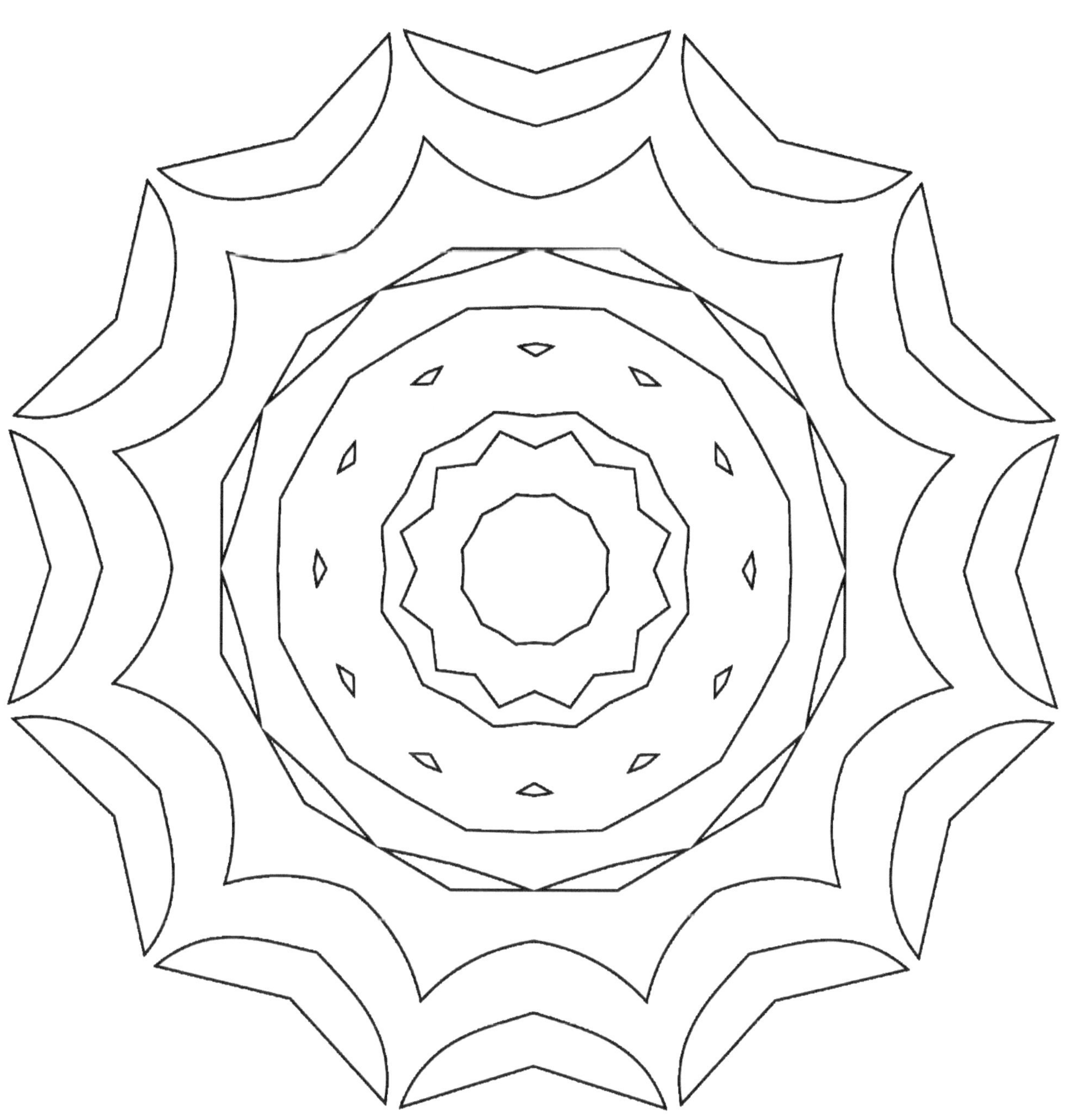

"It's the possibility of having a dream come true that makes life interesting."

— Paulo Coelho, The Alchemist

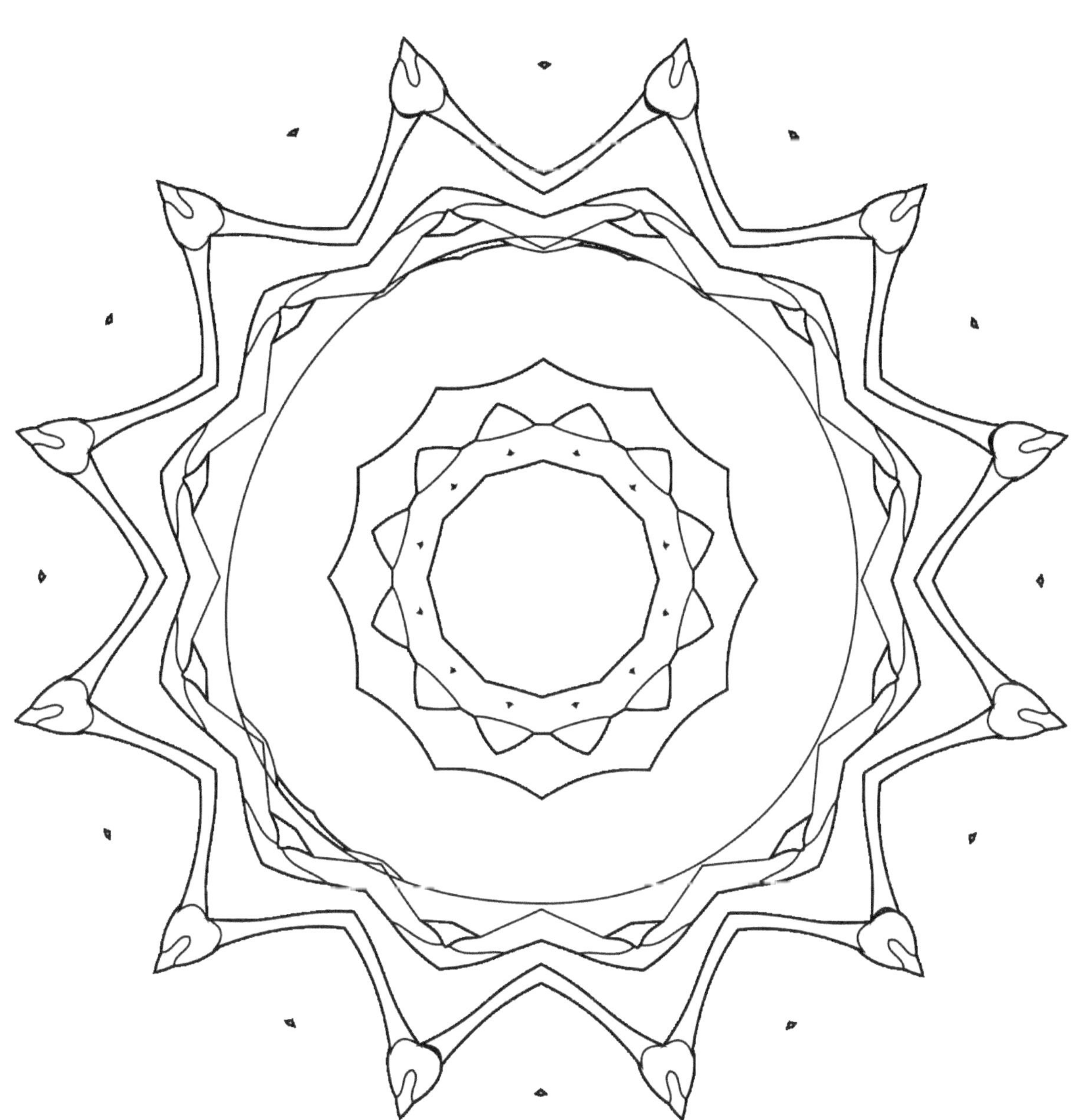

"Well-behaved women seldom make history."

— Laurel Thatcher Ulrich, Well-Behaved Women Seldom Make History

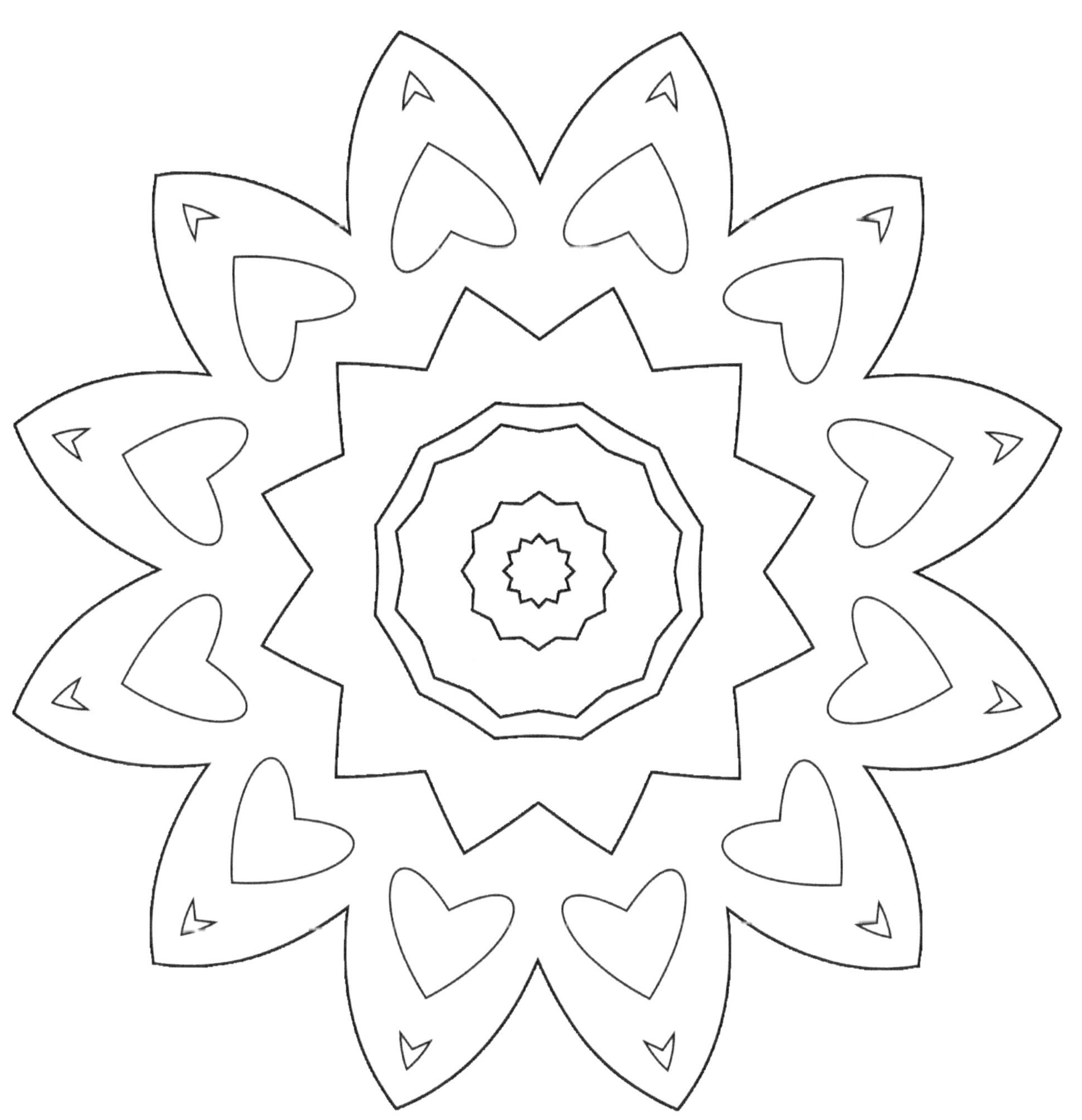

"Nothing is impossible, the word itself says 'I'm possible'!"

— Audrey Hepburn

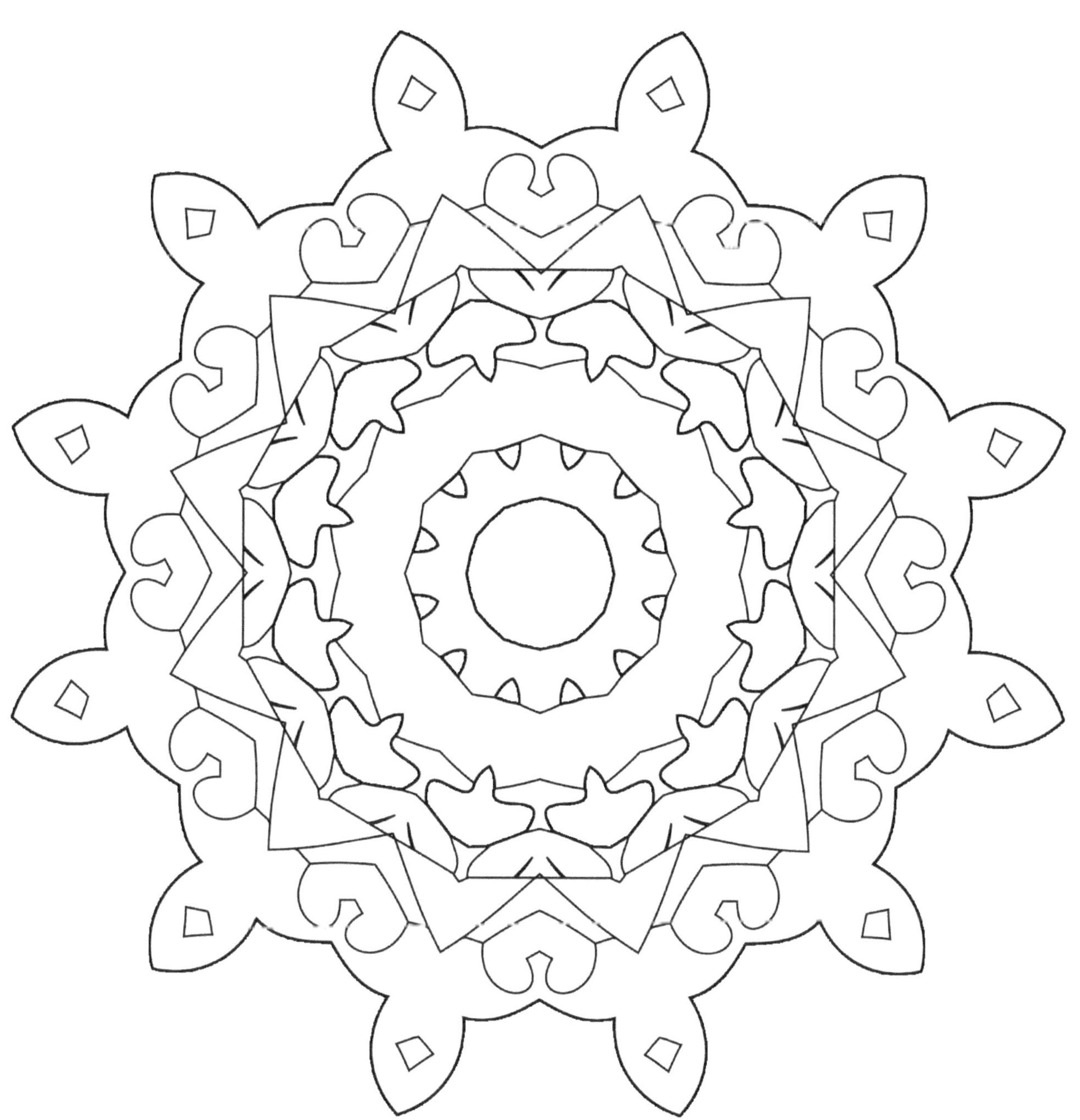

"I can't give you a sure-fire formula for success, but I can give you a formula for failure: try to please everybody all the time."

— Herbert Bayard Swope

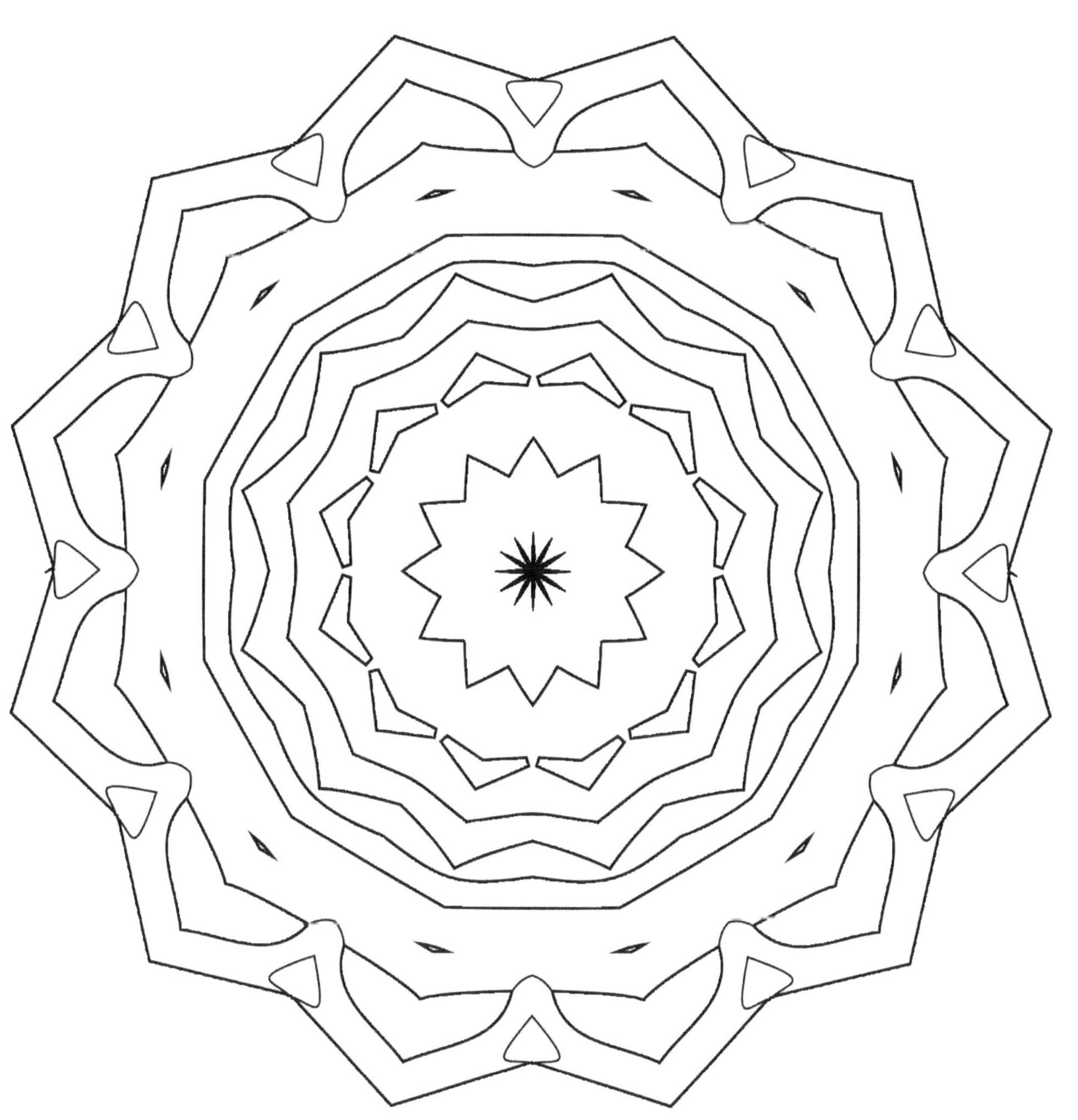

"When I despair, I remember that all through history the way of truth and love have always won. There have been tyrants and murderers, and for a time, they can seem invincible, but in the end, they always fall. Think of it--always."

— Mahatma Gandhi

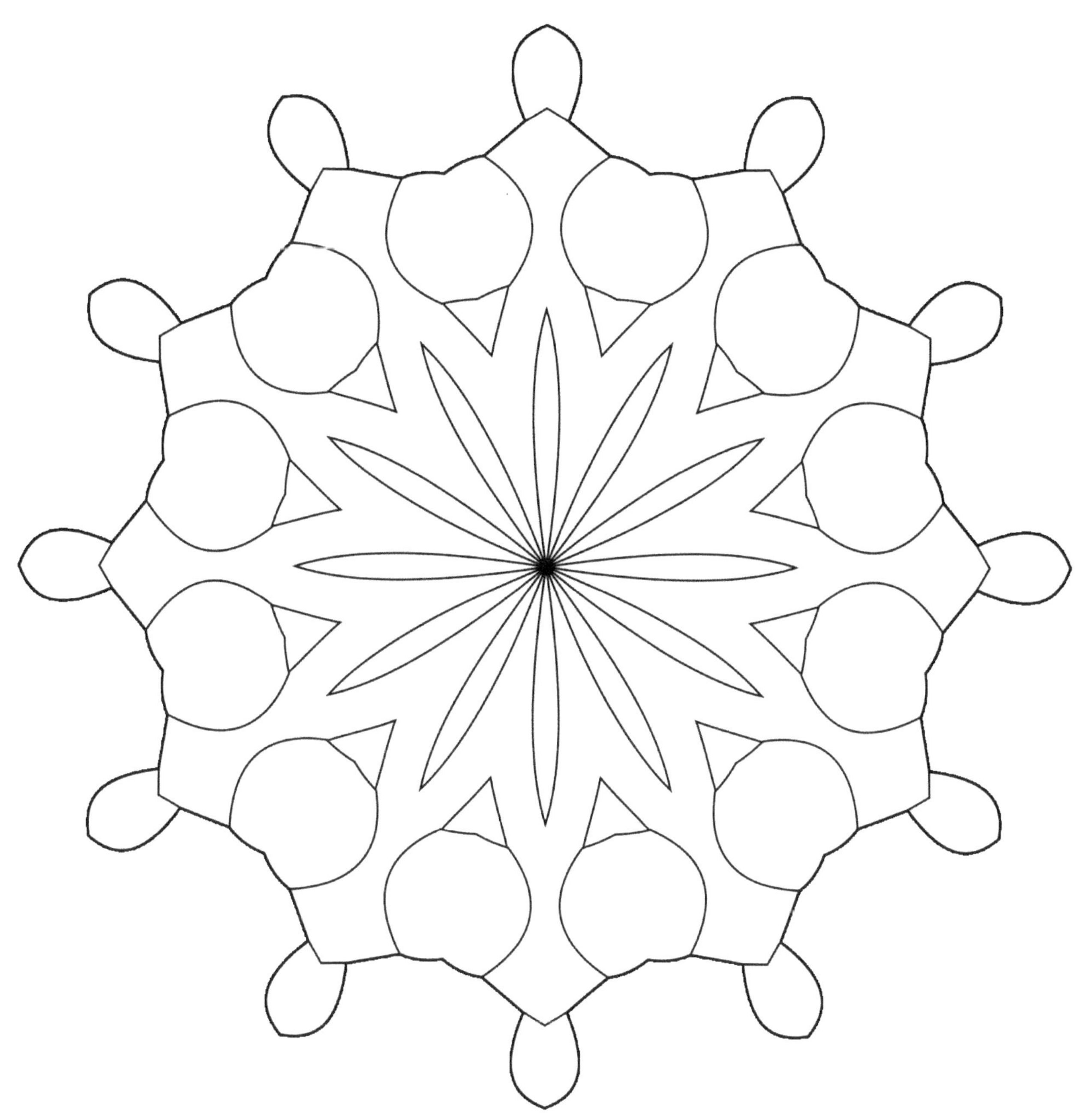

"Do what you feel in your heart to be right - for you'll be criticized anyway."

— Eleanor Roosevelt

"Peace begins with a smile.."

— Mother Teresa

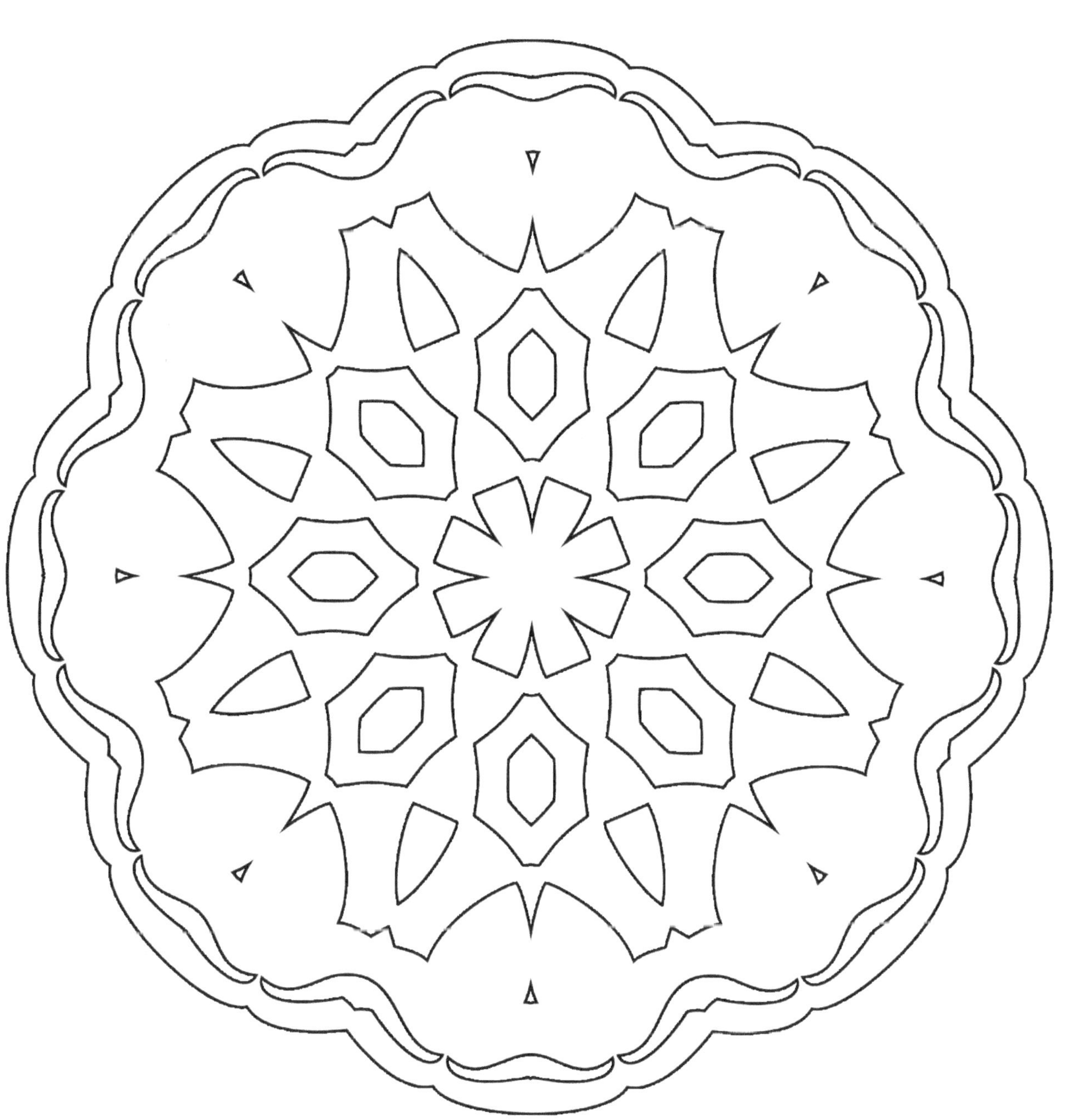

"Happiness is not something ready made. It comes from your own actions."

— Dalai Lama XIV

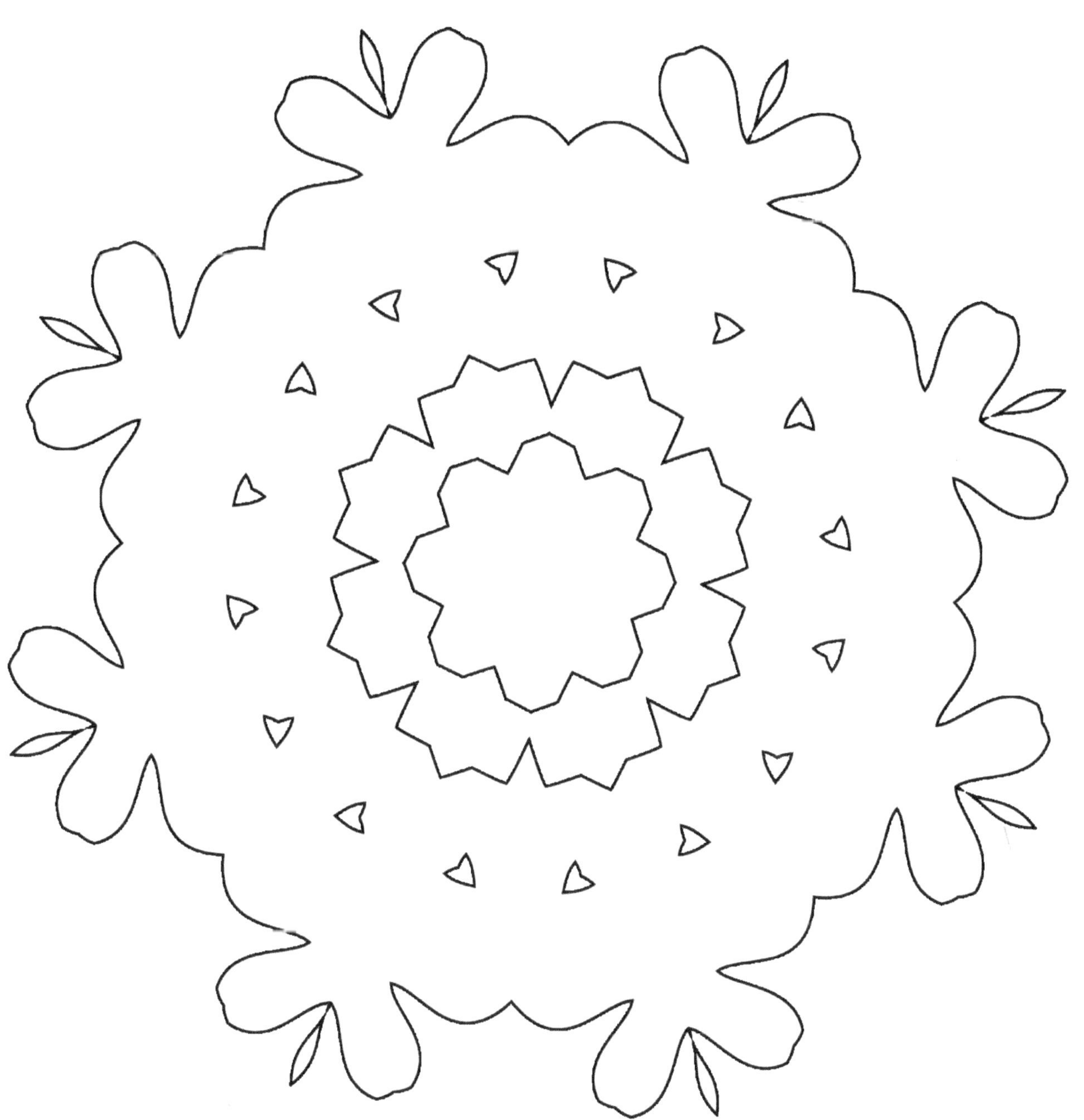

"Imagining the future is a kind of nostalgia. (...) You spend your whole life stuck in the labyrinth, thinking about how you'll escape it one day, and how awesome it will be, and imagining that future keeps you going, but you never do it. You just use the future to escape the present."

— John Green, Looking for Alaska

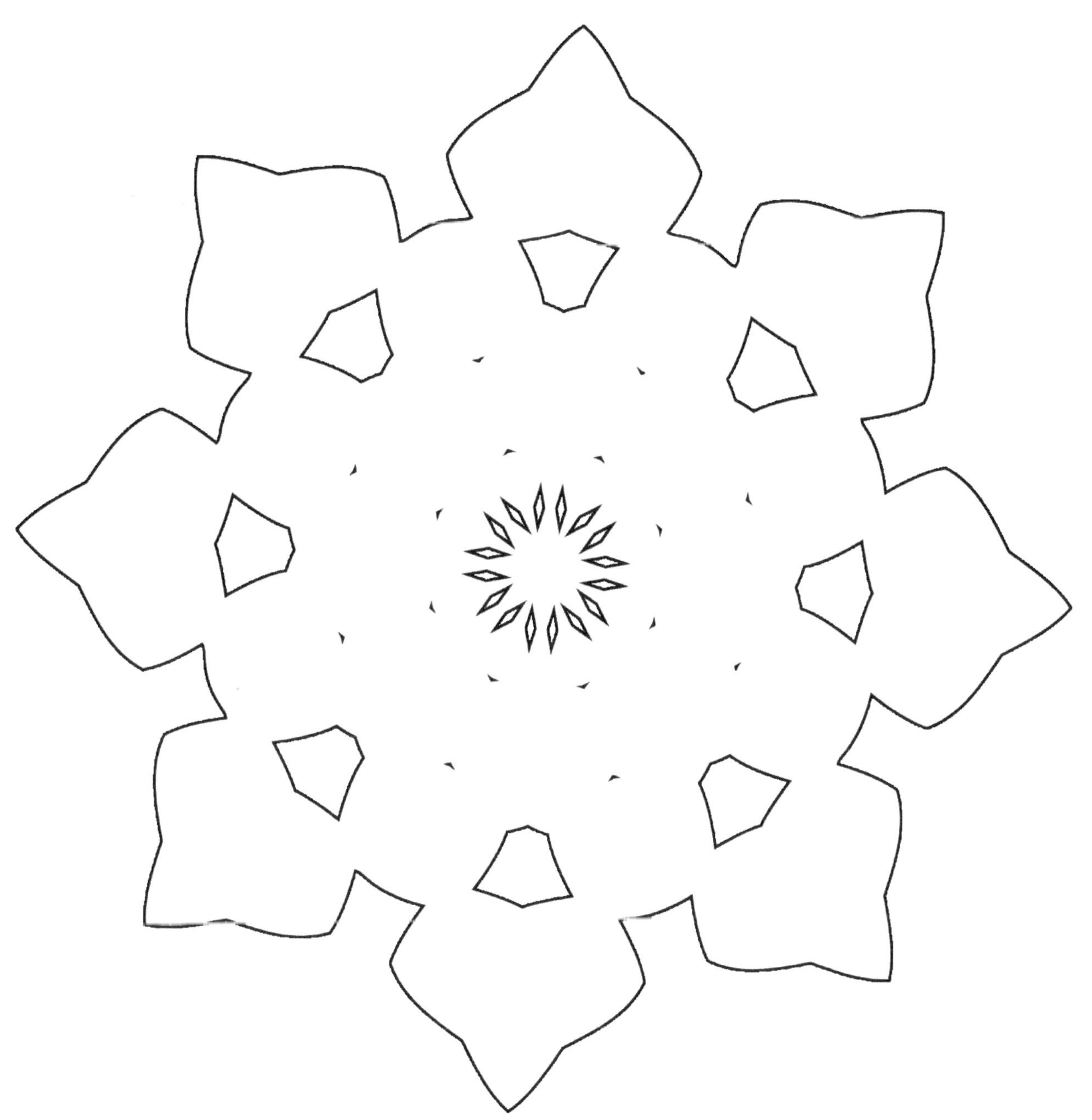

GET YOUR FREE COLORING PAGES

DON'T FORGET

Register and get your **FREE** pdf of **Coloring Pages**
:: www.DancingWithYourLife.com
And check out the full range of our books and products while you're there.

ALSO

Email us a photo of your proudest colored page from one of our coloring books to:
support@DancingWithYourLife.com

WIN A FREE COLORING BOOK

ones selected each month will be posted
/eb site and these **winners will get their choice of a free coloring book**

And to help others who may be considering this book, please share your experience with a brief review at:

www.ingramcontent.com/pod-product-compliance
Lightning Source LLC
LaVergne TN
LVHW081325110826
845149LV00007B/1595

* 9 7 8 0 9 9 4 4 2 3 0 2 3 *